CHINESE
MODERNIZATION:
THE WAY FORWARD

中国式现代化发展之路

中央党史和文献研究院国家高端智库
新华社国家高端智库联合课题组　著

新华出版社

图书在版编目（CIP）数据

中国式现代化发展之路：汉英对照 / 中央党史和文献研究院
国家高端智库，新华社国家高端智库联合课题组著．
-- 北京：新华出版社，2024.3
ISBN 978-7-5166-7391-1

Ⅰ．①中⋯ Ⅱ．①中⋯ ②新⋯ Ⅲ．①现代化建设—研究—中国—汉、英
Ⅳ．① D616

中国国家版本馆 CIP 数据核字（2024）第 083942 号

中国式现代化发展之路

作者： 中央党史和文献研究院国家高端智库、新华社国家高端智库联合课题组
出版发行： 新华出版社有限责任公司
（北京市石景山区京原路 8 号　邮编：100040）
印刷： 河北鑫兆源印刷有限公司

成品尺寸：170mm×240mm 1/16	印张：15.5	字数：150 千字
版次：2024 年 5 月第 1 版		印次：2024 年 5 月第 1 次印刷
书号：ISBN 978-7-5166-7391-1		定价：58.00 元

版权所有·侵权必究
如有印刷、装订问题，本公司负责调换。

微店

视频号小店

抖店

京东旗舰店

扫码添加专属客服

微信公众号

喜马拉雅

小红书

淘宝旗舰店

导　言 / 001

第一章　中国式现代化的发展历程 / 004

　　一、百年征程铸就时代新辉煌 / 005

　　二、中国式现代化改变了中国 / 011

第二章　中国式现代化的实践路径 / 017

　　一、中国共产党的领导是根本保障 / 018

　　二、坚持以人民为中心的发展思想 / 020

　　三、独立自主是必由之路 / 023

　　四、改革开放是关键一招 / 025

　　五、加快发展新质生产力 / 029

　　六、作为系统工程推进 / 033

第三章　中国式现代化的鲜明特色 / 037

　　一、人口规模巨大的现代化 / 038

　　二、全体人民共同富裕的现代化 / 043

　　三、物质文明和精神文明相协调的现代化 / 047

　　四、人与自然和谐共生的现代化 / 050

　　五、走和平发展道路的现代化 / 054

第四章　中国式现代化创造人类文明新形态 / 059

　　一、新价值形态：追求人民至上 / 060

　　二、新制度形态：不断完善革新 / 063

　　三、新发展形态：走向全面协调 / 066

　　四、新民主形态：全过程人民民主 / 069

　　五、新文化形态：坚持继承创新 / 072

　　六、新全球治理形态：构建人类命运共同体 / 075

结　语 / 079

编写说明与致谢 / 082

Chinese Modernization: The Way Forward

Introduction / 087

Chapter One The Evolution of Chinese Modernization / 090

1. Achievements on a Hundred-Year Journey / 091
2. Chinese Modernization Has Changed China / 098

Chapter Two Practical Approaches to Chinese Modernization / 103

1. Leadership by the CPC Is the Fundamental Underpinning of Chinese Modernization / 104
2. Upholding a People-Centered Development Philosophy / 106
3. Independence and Self-Reliance Are the Only Way / 109
4. Reform and Opening Up Is a Crucial Move / 110
5. Accelerating the Development of New Quality Productive Forces / 115
6. Advancing Chinese Modernization as a Systematic Endeavor / 119

Chapter Three Defining Features of Chinese Modernization / 124

1. Modernization of a Large Population / 125
2. Modernization for the Common Prosperity of All / 130
3. Modernization of Material and Cultural-ethical Advancement / 134
4. Modernization of Harmony Between Humanity and Nature / 138
5. Modernization of Peaceful Development / 142

Chapter Four Chinese Modernization: A New Form of Human Advancement / 147

1. A New Form of Values: Putting the People First / 148

2. A New Form of System: Constant Improvement and Reform / 151

3. A New Form of Development: Becoming More Comprehensive and Coordinated / 154

4. A New Form of Democracy: Whole-process People's Democracy / 157

5. A New Form of Culture: Continually Learning From the Past to Make Innovations / 160

6. A New Form of Global Governance: Building a Human Community with a Shared Future / 164

Conclusion / 168

新华社大型纪录片《难以置信的变化：一个美国人眼中的中国式现代化》

第一集　润物细无声 / 174

第二集　同欲者胜之 / 189

第三集　上下而求索 / 204

第四集　天地我同根 / 217

第五集　相知无远近 / 229

导 言

18世纪中期,"珍妮纺纱机"拉开了工业革命的大幕,西方国家从此开启了现代化进程。

两百五十多年过去了,现代化大潮依然滚滚向前。曾经灾难深重、风雨飘摇的中国,正在中国共产党的领导下踏上充满光荣与梦想的现代化新征程。

中国式现代化,是中国共产党领导的社会主义现代化,既有各国现代化的共同特征,更有基于自己国情的鲜明特色:它是人口规模巨大的现代化,全体人民共同富裕的现代化,物质文明和精神文明相协调的现代化,人与自然和谐共生的现代化,走和平发展道路的现代化。

世界上是否存在定于一尊的现代化模式?有没有放之四海而皆准的现代化标准?本报告用中国式现代化的理论和实践作

出了否定的回答。

立足历史的纵深发展，报告探究了中国共产党带领中国人民实现现代化的百年脉络、卓绝探索。新中国成立以来，特别是中共十八大以来，中国在科技发展、经济和生态文明建设等领域取得了享誉世界的巨大成就。

报告总结了中国式现代化的实践路径：在中国共产党领导下，坚持以人民为中心的发展思想，独立自主走自己的路，用好改革开放关键一招，加快发展新质生产力，实现科技自立自强，系统推进现代化各项事业。在全世界最大的马克思主义执政党的坚强领导下，中国将成为全球探索绿色低碳高质量发展的先行者、构建人类命运共同体的实践者和沉着冷静应对百年未有之大变局的实干者。

报告分析认为，中国式现代化，创造了人类文明新形态。不同于西方式现代化，中国式现代化在价值取向上摒弃资本至上、追求人民至上，在制度建设上证伪"历史终结论"、不断完善革新；在发展路径上走出"单向""异化"、走向全面协调；在民主形态上不搞少数人民主、实现人民当家作主；在文化认同上从不割裂传统、坚持继承创新；在全球治理上不搞单边主义、推动构建人类命运共同体。

报告指出，现代化不仅是经济的现代化，也是人的全面发展的现代化。中国式现代化树立了发展中国家独立自主迈向现代化的典范，探索出了一条发展中国家走向现代化的途径。中国式现代化的理论和实践，为那些既希望加快发展，又希望保持独立性的国家和民族提供了全新的选择，为更多发展中国家探索适合本国国情的现代化道路带来了希望、增强了信心、提供了启示。

道阻且长，行则将至；日出东方，其道大光。

第一章

中国式现代化的发展历程

中国共产党一经诞生,就把为中国人民谋幸福、为中华民族谋复兴确立为自己的初心使命。一百年来,中国共产党团结带领中国人民进行的一切奋斗、一切牺牲、一切创造,归结起来就是一个主题:实现中华民族伟大复兴。[①]

——习近平

1921年,嘉兴南湖,一叶红船扬起了中国现代化百年征程的风帆。"作始也简,将毕也钜",无声,却似惊雷,中国共产党的成立为波澜壮阔的奋斗史诗写下了光辉的起笔。从石库门到天安门,从兴业路到复兴路,我们党百年来所付出的一切

---

① 《习近平:在庆祝中国共产党成立100周年大会上的讲话》,新华社,2021年7月1日。

努力、进行的一切斗争、作出的一切牺牲，都是为了人民幸福和民族复兴。百年风华正茂，一代又一代中国共产党人带领中国人民、中华民族在追求中国式现代化道路上步步探索、前行，推动中国式现代化事业取得举世瞩目的伟大成就，为人类进步事业作出灿烂辉煌的卓越贡献。

一、百年征程铸就时代新辉煌

在人类社会发展中，中华民族创造了悠久灿烂的中华文明，长期屹立于世界民族之林，为人类文明进步作出了不可磨灭的贡献。但17世纪中叶后，西方一些国家先后爆发资产阶级革命，并相继完成工业革命，在新的生产方式推动下迅速强大起来，资产阶级开始了血与火的原始积累和殖民掠夺。

幅员辽阔、资源丰富、人口众多的中国，在世界近代化、工业化、现代化的大潮中逐渐落伍，自然成为西方列强垂涎和争夺的市场。从1840年开始，西方列强不断发动侵略战争，强迫中国割地、赔款，贪婪地攫取种种特权，严重抑制了中国经济发展和现代化进程。

"国家蒙辱、人民蒙难、文明蒙尘"[①]是对这一时期中国被迫卷入西方主导的现代化浪潮的深刻总结。无数仁人志士历经

---

① 《习近平：在庆祝中国共产党成立100周年大会上的讲话》，新华社，2021年7月1日。

千辛万苦，尝试向西方国家学习先进的制度和技术，追求中国的富强进步之路。以曾国藩、李鸿章、左宗棠、张之洞等为代表的洋务派，康有为、梁启超为代表的维新派，以孙中山、黄兴为代表的革命派在近代中国追求现代化的进程中以百折不挠的精神，不断尝试各种救国方案，但最终都以失败告终，没能改变旧中国积贫积弱的面貌。

十月革命一声炮响，给中国送来了马克思列宁主义。此后，中国追求现代化的重任，历史地落在了中国共产党人身上。在一代又一代中国共产党人的带领下，中华民族迎来了从站起来、富起来到强起来的伟大飞跃。中国现代化进程实现了从被迫卷入西方现代化到以中国式现代化新道路引领世界现代化新潮流的历史性转变。

（一）1921—1949年：新民主主义革命时期的现代化初探

山河破碎、任人宰割之时，1921年，中国共产党成立了，中国人民有了改变苦难和屈辱的希望。

在实践和探索中，早期中国共产党人认识到，新的生产力不可能建立在帝国主义、封建主义和官僚资本主义基础上，中国首先需要一场伟大的社会革命。中国的现代化必须以争取民族独立和人民解放为根本前提和基础。

这一时期，中国共产党团结带领中国人民进行新民主主义革命，建立了人民当家作主的新中国，实现了民族独立、人民解放，彻底结束了旧中国半殖民地半封建社会的历史，彻底结束了极少数剥削者统治广大劳动人民的历史，彻底结束了旧中国一盘散沙的局面，彻底废除了列强强加给中国的不平等条约和帝国主义在中国的一切特权，实现了中国从几千年专制政治向人民民主的伟大飞跃，为中国实现现代化创造了根本社会条件。

（二）1949—1978年：社会主义革命和建设时期的现代化探索

中华人民共和国的成立，是中国由近代衰落走向强盛的历史转折点，它为中国朝着社会主义方向和国家现代化目标迈进创造了前提。

新中国是在一穷二白基础上建立起来的，中国当时极其缺乏大机器制造业和现代技术装备。毛泽东曾经形象地说："现在我们能造什么？能造桌子椅子，能造茶碗茶壶，能种粮食，还能磨成面粉，还能造纸，但是，一辆汽车、一架飞机、一辆坦克、一辆拖拉机都不能造。"

1953年12月，毛泽东提出建设"现代化工业""农业和交通运输业的现代化""现代化的国防"，初步提出实现"四个现代化"的思想。1954年9月，周恩来代表中共中央第一次明确提出了建设现代化的工业、现代化的农业、现代化的交通运输业和现代化的国防的要求。在1964年底至1965年初召开的第三届全国人民代表大会第一次会议上，周恩来正式向全国人民公布了实现农业、工业、国防和科学技术四个现代化的战略目标。

为了实现"四个现代化"战略目标，中共中央在1964年提出了"两步走"的发展规划：第一步，建立一个独立的比较完整的工业体系和国民经济体系；第二步，全面实现农业、工业、国防和科学技术的现代化，使中国经济走在世界前列。

经过中国人民的艰苦奋斗，到20世纪70年代末，中国建立起了独立的比较完整的工业体系和国民经济体系，实现了"四个现代化"的第一步发展战略。这一阶段取得的独创性理论成果和巨大成就，为中国现代化建设提供了宝贵经验、理论准备、物质基础。

（三）1978—2012年：改革开放新时期的现代化新局面

20世纪70年代末，随着新一轮科技革命的兴起，世界范围内的现代化加速发展。国内外发展大势都要求中国共产党尽快就关系党和国家前途命运的大政方针作出政治决断和战略抉择。1978年12月，中国共产党召开十一届三中全会，作出把党和国家工作中心转移到经济建设上来、实行改革开放的历史性决策。1979年3月，邓小平从实际出发，创造性地提出"中国式的现代化"。当年12月，他还用富有中华传统文化特色的"小康"来诠释中国式现代化，明确了20世纪末中国能够达到的现代化水平，由此，"小康"成为中国推进现代化道路上的一面鲜明旗帜。1987年，中共中央制定了"三步走"现代化发展战略：第一步，到20世纪80年代末解决人民温饱问题；第二步，到20世纪末使人民生活达到小康水平；第三步，到21世纪中叶基本实现现代化，达到中等发达国家水平。

为加快推进中国式的现代化，中国共产党人大胆探索，成功把社会主义制度和市场经济结合起来，确立了社会主义市场经济体制的改革目标，改革开放和现代化建设进入新的阶段。2001年12月11日，中国正式加入世界贸易组织，深度融入全球化进程，这是我国改革开放和社会主义现代化建设进程中的一个重要里程碑。中国积极主动与世界贸易组织规则接轨，推动贸易自由化和投资便利化，在扩大开放的同时，也为经济全球化向前发展注入了强劲动力，激活了世界经济的"一池春水"。

这一时期，中国实现了从生产力相对落后到经济总量跃居世界第二的历史性突破，实现了人民生活从温饱不足到总体小康、奔向全面小康的历史性跨越，为中国式现代化提供了充满新的活力的体制保证和快速发展的物质条件。

（四）2012年至今：新时代的中国式现代化全面展开

2012年11月，中共十八大召开，中国特色社会主义进入新时代，中国式现代化全面展开。以习近平同志为核心的中共中央在全面总结、充分吸收中国现代化建设经验的基础上，不断拓展中国式现代化的理论内涵，不断推进中国式现代化的实践发展，开辟了以中国式现代化全面推进中华民族伟大复兴的新境界。

——在认识上，深化了对中国式现代化的内涵和本质的认识，概括形成了中国式现代化的中国特色、本质要求和重大原则，初步构建起中国式现代化的理论体系，使中国式现代化更加清晰、更加科学、更加可感可行。中国正在经历的新时代，是一个不可逆转地实现中华民族伟大复兴的历史进程，在此历史背景下应运而生的习近平新时代中国特色社会主义思想，实现了马克思主义中国化时代化新的飞跃，为中国式现代化提供了根本遵循。

——在战略上，确定分"两步走"全面建成社会主义现代化强国的时间表，即从二〇二〇年到二〇三五年基本实现社会主义现代化；从二〇三五年到本世纪中叶把中国建成富强民主文明和谐美丽的社会主义现代化强国。经济建设、政治建设、文化建设、社会建设、生态文明建设的"五位一体"总体布局和全面建设社会主义现代化国家、全面深化改革、全面依法治国、全面从严治党的"四个全面"战略布局渐次铺开，科教兴国战略、人才强国战略、乡村振兴战略等一系列重大战略深入推进，为中国式现代化提供坚实支撑。

——在实践上，以习近平同志为核心的中共中央团结带领全党全国人民不懈奋斗，推动新时代党和国家事业取得历史性成就、发生历史性变革，特别是解决了困扰中华民族几千年的绝对贫困问题，如期实现第一个百年奋斗目标，全面建成小康社会，创造了人类减贫史上的奇迹，朝着实现全体人民共同富裕的目标迈出坚实的一步。

推进中国式现代化是一项前无古人的开创性事业，新时代推进的一系列变革性实践、实现的一系列突破性进展、取得的一系列标志性成果，为中国式现代化提供更为完善的制度保证、更为坚实的物质基础、更为主动的精神力量。

经过一百多年的不懈奋斗，中国式现代化道路已走出一片天地并获初步成功。中国式现代化理论及其实践从中国具体实际出发，赋予马克思主义发展理论新的时代内涵，融合吸收中华优秀传统文化精髓，呈现出不同于西方现代化的理论认知。中国式现代化，打破了"现代化＝西方化"的迷思，丰富和发展了世界现代化理论的知识图景。

"惟其艰巨，所以伟大；惟其艰巨，更显荣光"，在接续推进中国式现代化新的赶考路上，中国共产党一定能团结带领中国人民交出一份经得起历史检验的答卷。

二、中国式现代化改变了中国

中国共产党领导中国人民用几十年时间走完了西方发达国家几百年走过的工业化历程，中国式现代化事业取得了举世瞩目的辉煌成就，书写了经济快速发展和社会长期稳定"两大奇迹"。中国从一个积贫积弱的落后国家，一跃成为世界第二大经济体，综合国力实现历史性跨越。

（一）完成脱贫攻坚，实现全面小康千年梦想

小康是中华民族的千年梦想和夙愿。中共十八大以来，中国共产党把脱贫攻坚摆在治国理政突出位置，充分发挥党的领导和社会主义制度的政治优势，采取了许多具有原创性、独特性的重大举措，组织实施了人类历史上规模最大、力度最强的脱贫攻坚战。经过8年持续奋斗，中国如期完成了新时代脱贫攻坚目标任务，到2020年底，实现了中国现行标准下9899万农村贫困人口全部脱贫，832个贫困县全部摘帽，12.8万个贫困村全部出列，区域性整体贫困得到解决。[1]

2021年7月1日，在庆祝中国共产党成立100周年大会上，习近平庄严宣告，经过全党全国各族人民持续奋斗，我们实现了第一个百年奋斗目标，在中华大地上全面建成了小康社会，历史性地解决了绝对贫困问题，正在意气风发向着全面建成社会主义现代化强国的第二个百年奋斗目标迈进。全面建成小康社会，实现了中国现代化建设的阶段性目标，中华民族伟大复兴迈出了关键一步。

中国的减贫成就也对世界作出了突出的贡献，对全球减贫

---

[1]《习近平：在全国脱贫攻坚总结表彰大会上的讲话》，新华社，2021年2月25日。

贡献率达到70%以上，在人类历史发展中具有重要的里程碑意义。[1]同时，中国的精准扶贫推动了扶贫减贫理论创新和实践创新，对全球面临类似挑战的国家具有借鉴意义，标志着人类社会消灭贫困的方式已经超越了资本主义的限定，世界历史将在实现人类真正平等的事业上翻开全新的一页。

（二）经济快速发展，国内生产总值历史性飞跃

中共十八大以来，中国经济实现历史性跃升，国内生产总值（GDP）从2012年的53.9万亿元增长到2023年的126万亿元，按年平均汇率折算，经济总量约18万亿美元，稳居世界第二位，对世界经济增长的平均贡献率达30%以上。

——经济量质齐升带动全球经济增长。十多年来，中国从制造大国加快转向制造强国，服务业稳居国民经济第一大产业，绿色成为经济发展鲜亮底色，消费成为拉动经济第一大引擎，城镇化率稳步提高，粮食安全、能源安全和人民生活得到有效保障，"三新"（新产业、新业态、新商业模式）经济增加值占GDP比重已超过17%。2012年至2021年，中国经济总量占世界经济比重从11.4%提升到18%以上。过去十年，中国对全球经济增长的带动超过七国集团总和。

---

[1] 王治东：《新中国70年发展成就具有世界历史意义》，《光明日报》2019年10月16日，第6版。

——建设高水平开放型经济格局。近年来，中国不断降低关税总水平，持续放宽市场准入，对外开放范围、领域和层次持续拓展，外贸方式不断创新，外资市场准入进一步放宽，高水平开放型经济格局加快形成，中国开放的大门越开越大，促进了全球发展繁荣。中国已经是140多个国家和地区的主要贸易伙伴，[①]是越来越多国家的主要投资来源地。在世界经济复苏动力不足的今天，稳步提升的中国经济为充满不确定性的世界带来难得的确定性，为全球经济复苏注入更强劲动能。

（三）活力与秩序、发展与稳定相平衡，亿万人民共襄国泰民安

在实现经济快速发展的同时，中国共产党以共同富裕为价值导向，注重处理效率和公平的关系，实现活力与秩序、发展与稳定相平衡，满足亿万人民国泰民安的普遍愿望，为以中国式现代化全面推进中华民族伟大复兴创造良好社会环境，为世界和平提供了稳定性和建设性因素。

——国家安全全面加强。面对更为严峻的国内国际形势，中国贯彻总体国家安全观，不断完善国家安全领导体制和法治体系、战略体系、政策体系，以高质量发展夯实高水平安全物

[①]《习近平在第三届"一带一路"国际合作高峰论坛开幕式上的主旨演讲》，新华社，2023年10月18日。

质基础，以高水平安全保障高质量发展，实现高质量发展和高水平安全的良性互动。深化反恐怖反分裂斗争，连续6年保持暴恐案事件"零发生"[①]。推动实现港澳地区长治久安和"一国两制"行稳致远。通过综合施策、持续努力，有效增强全社会维护国家安全的积极性主动性，进一步巩固各领域安全的人民防线。

——人民生活全方位改善。中国共产党以保障和改善民生为重点加强社会建设，尽力而为、量力而行，一件事情接着一件事情办，一年接着一年干，在幼有所育、学有所教、劳有所得、病有所医、老有所养、住有所居、弱有所扶上持续用力。1949年以来，中国人均预期寿命从不足35岁增长到78.2岁，人民受教育程度从文盲率高达80%到减少至2.67%，人民群众的获得感、幸福感、安全感得到有效保障。中共十八大以来，中国解决了1.3亿余人的城镇就业问题，建成世界上规模最大的教育体系、社会保障体系、医疗卫生体系。

——国家治理体系和治理能力现代化不断提升。截至2022年底，中国加快推进社会治理体制改革，尤其是中共十八大以来，从"加强和创新社会管理"到"创新社会治理体制"，从构建"社会治理新格局"到打造"社会治理共同体"，治理主体日益多

[①] 《公安部：我国连续6年保持暴恐案事件"零发生"》，人民网，2023年1月10日，http://society.people.com.cn/n1/2023/0110/c1008-32603569.htm。

元多样,彰显了人人有责、人人尽责、人人享有的原则。到2021年底,全国城市社区综合服务设施覆盖率由"十三五"末的82%到实现全覆盖,农村社区综合服务设施覆盖率由31.8%上升到84.6%,将争取"十四五"末实现城乡社区综合服务设施全覆盖。

第二章

中国式现代化的实践路径

实践证明，中国式现代化走得通、行得稳，是强国建设、民族复兴的唯一正确道路。①

——习近平

中国式现代化的成功，不是从天上掉下来的，也不是从地下冒出来的，而是中国共产党秉持初心使命，团结带领中国人民一步一个脚印走出来的，一关接着一关闯出来的，一代接着一代干出来的。

中国共产党在领导推进中国式现代化的实践中，坚持对中

---

① 《习近平在学习贯彻党的二十大精神研讨班开班式上发表重要讲话强调 正确理解和大力推进中国式现代化 李强主持 赵乐际王沪宁蔡奇丁薛祥李希出席》，新华社，2023年2月7日。

国式现代化事业的全面领导、坚持以人民为中心的发展思想、坚持走独立自主道路、坚持改革开放、坚持发展新质生产力、坚持系统推进，确保中国式现代化行稳致远。

一、中国共产党的领导是根本保障

中国式现代化是中国共产党领导的社会主义现代化。党的领导直接关系中国式现代化的根本方向、前途命运、最终成败，是中国式现代化行稳致远的根本保障。

（一）确保中国式现代化在正确轨道上顺利推进

旗帜决定方向，方向决定道路，道路决定命运。举什么旗、走什么路，是一个国家发展的根本性问题。中国共产党高举中国特色社会主义伟大旗帜，坚定不移走中国特色社会主义道路，确保中国式现代化在正确轨道上顺利前进。

中国共产党不断推进实践基础上的理论创新，为中国式现代化提供科学理论指引；不断推进国家治理体系和治理能力现代化，为中国式现代化提供坚强制度保证；不断推进中华优秀传统文化创造性转化、创新性发展，建设中华民族现代文明，为中国式现代化提供强大精神力量。

习近平强调："只有毫不动摇坚持党的领导，中国式现代化才能前景光明、繁荣兴盛；否则就会偏离航向、丧失灵魂，甚至犯颠覆性错误。"①

（二）确保锚定中国式现代化奋斗目标行稳致远

中国共产党坚守为人民谋幸福、为民族谋复兴的初心使命，坚持把远大理想与阶段性目标统一起来，一旦确定目标，就咬定青山不放松，一张蓝图绘到底，从根本上超越了一些国家政党纷争不断、政策朝令夕改的弊端。

推进中国式现代化是一场历史接力赛。特别是改革开放以来，中国追求现代化的奋斗目标一以贯之、循序渐进，随着实践发展而不断丰富完善。中共二十大擘画了全面建成社会主义现代化强国、以中国式现代化全面推进中华民族伟大复兴的宏伟蓝图。这种锚定奋斗目标一代接着一代干的精神，深刻体现了中国共产党的战略定力和制度优势。

（三）凝聚建设中国式现代化的磅礴力量

一盘散沙没有希望，团结统一才有力量。在中国这样一个人口众多、国情复杂的大国，要把各方面力量团结起来建设现代化，首先要有一个团结统一的党。

---

① 《习近平在学习贯彻党的二十大精神研讨班开班式上发表重要讲话强调 正确理解和大力推进中国式现代化 李强主持 赵乐际王沪宁蔡奇丁薛祥李希出席》，新华社，2023年2月7日。

中国共产党从一个几十人的小党逐步发展为拥有9800多万名党员、在14亿多人口大国长期执政的百年大党，始终高度重视依靠共同的理想信念、严密的组织体系、全党的高度自觉、严明的纪律规矩来实现党的团结统一。中国共产党坚持用马克思主义中国化时代化最新成果武装全党，使全党统一思想、统一意志、统一行动。

中国式现代化是亿万人民自己的事业，人民是中国式现代化的主体。中国共产党根基在人民、血脉在人民、力量在人民，没有任何自己特殊的利益，不代表任何利益集团、任何权势团体、任何特权阶层，始终代表最广大人民的根本利益。中国共产党以中国式现代化的美好愿景激励人、鼓舞人、感召人，有效促进政党关系、民族关系、宗教关系、阶层关系、海内外同胞关系和谐，促进海内外中华儿女团结奋斗，凝聚起全面建设社会主义现代化国家的磅礴伟力。

二、坚持以人民为中心的发展思想

发展是人类社会的永恒主题。现代化顺应了人类对美好生活的向往，是世界各国孜孜以求的目标。中国式现代化坚持以人民为中心的发展思想，维护人民利益，增进人民福祉，不断实现发展为了人民、发展依靠人民、发展成果由人民共享，让现代化建设成果更多更公平惠及全体人民。

（一）坚持把发展作为执政兴国的第一要务

现代化的目标要靠发展来实现。中国共产党坚持"发展是党执政兴国的第一要务"，强调"发展才是硬道理""发展是解决中国一切问题的总钥匙""聚精会神搞建设，一心一意谋发展"，将发展作为推进中国式现代化的主线。

在世界现代化进程中，中国式现代化是后发式现代化。后发赶超并非易事，成功国家屈指可数。许多后发国家在追求现代化的道路上，陷入了各种各样的发展困境。归根到底，如何保持经济持续健康发展，是一个世界性难题。

改革开放以来，经过 40 多年快速发展，中国经济总量快速攀升，目前已经稳居世界第二位。2023 年，中国人均国内生产总值 89358 元，比上年增长 5.4%，按年平均汇率折算达 1.27 万美元，连续 3 年保持在 1.2 万美元以上，[①] 中国经济取得了举世瞩目的发展成就。

（二）不断满足人民日益增长的美好生活需要

治国有常，利民为本。中国式现代化践行以人民为中心的发展思想，坚持发展为了人民、发展依靠人民、发展成果由人民共享，不断满足人民日益增长的美好生活需要，让现代化成

---

① 中共国家统计局党组：《我国经济回升向好、长期向好的基本趋势没有改变》，《求是》2024 年第 3 期。

果更多更公平惠及全体人民。

江山就是人民，人民就是江山。打江山、守江山，守的是人民的心。习近平强调，"人民对美好生活的向往，就是我们的奋斗目标"，"共产党就是给人民办事的，就是要让人民的生活一天天好起来，一年比一年过得好"。

在这样的理念指引下，中国高度重视在发展中保障和改善民生，采取有力有效举措，解决好同老百姓生活息息相关的教育、就业、医疗卫生、社会保障、社会稳定等民生问题，不断提升人民群众获得感、幸福感、安全感。

（三）把握"三新一高"中国发展大逻辑

中国式现代化是进行时，而不是完成时。实践证明，中国式现代化是强国建设、民族复兴的康庄大道。但康庄大道不等于一马平川，不可能一蹴而就。把中国式现代化的宏伟蓝图变为成功实践，还需付出艰巨努力。

新征程上，如何继续书写发展奇迹？中国提出了"三新一高"发展逻辑：立足新发展阶段、贯彻新发展理念、构建新发展格局、推动高质量发展。即立足全面建设社会主义现代化国家的新发展阶段，深入贯彻创新、协调、绿色、开放、共享的新发展理念，加快构建以国内大循环为主体、国内国际双循环相互促进的新发展格局，持续推动高质量发展。

新发展阶段锚定了历史方位，新发展理念确立了指导原则，新发展格局指明了发展路径，三者统一于高质量发展这个主题。高质量发展是全面建设社会主义现代化国家的首要任务。中国过去发展更多是解决"有没有"的问题，未来发展将更加重视解决"好不好"的问题，不断提升发展质量和效益。

三、独立自主是必由之路

中国式现代化是中国共产党团结带领中国人民独立自主、长期探索、不懈奋斗走出来的适合中国国情、满足中国人民需要的独特道路。这是由中国国情和国家性质以及中国式现代化所处的时代条件、历史方位、外部环境所决定的。

（一）依靠中国共产党坚强领导，团结奋斗实现现代化

中国人口规模巨大，是一个拥有14亿多人口的发展中国家，要在现代化的进程中实现全体人民的共同富裕，必然面对纷繁复杂的矛盾和问题。要处理和解决这些矛盾和问题，依靠中国共产党的坚强领导、依靠全体中国人民的团结奋斗是我们唯一正确的选择。只有充分发挥社会主义制度的政治优势，才能有效调动各方面积极性，集中力量办大事，汇聚起现代化建设的强大合力。

（二）依靠全体中国人民艰辛探索，蹚出自己的路

一些发展中国家曾寄希望于模仿、复制西方道路来实现本国现代化，但最终都以失败告终，其原因在于这种模仿和复制忽视了本国实际。上世纪80年代后，一些拉美国家全盘接受"华盛顿共识"的政策建议，不同程度推行了新自由主义改革，虽然经济转型取得一些成效，但很快也产生了一系列严重问题，如国家失去对经济控制力、社会两极分化加剧等。

与之不同的是，中国的现代化一直坚持走自己的路，坚持与中国的具体实际相结合，通过不断艰辛探索，明确中国式现代化的目标任务、基本特征、本质要求等，具有鲜明的中国特色，是扎根中国国情实际，逐步探索形成的适合本国国情的现代化发展之路。

（三）唯有独立自主，才能避免受制于人

要自强必先独立，将自己的国家命脉、前途命运交到他人手里，不仅现代化会成为泡影，甚至可能最终导致任人宰割、崩溃灭亡的结果。一百多年来，中国共产党团结带领中国人民坚持不懈、接力奋斗，战胜一个又一个难以想象的困难，取得一个又一个重大的胜利。在经济持续发展、14亿多人民生活水平持续提高、实现全面小康的同时，中国共产党的执政地位更加巩固，中国特色社会主义的航船行稳致远。这一切成就的取得，都是在独立自主的条件下实现的。

四、改革开放是关键一招

纵观世界现代化发展史，经济现代化既是国家现代化的核心内容和物质基础，也是整个现代化的重要动力源。1978年拉开帷幕的中国改革开放，是中国大踏步赶上时代的重要法宝，是决定当代中国命运的关键一招，对继续推进中国式现代化有至关重要的意义。

（一）没有改革开放，就没有中国的今天

改革开放前，中国一度陷入僵化，落后于时代。中国社会主义改革开放和现代化建设的总设计师邓小平以极大政治勇气力主中国实行改革开放。他说："如果现在再不实行改革，我们的现代化事业和社会主义事业就会被葬送。"邓小平把改革开放作为解放和发展生产力的重要途径，和中国社会主义的前途命运联系起来。改革开放后，中国共产党带领中国人民解放思想、实事求是，大胆地试、勇敢地改，不断调整不适应生产力发展的生产关系，大踏步赶上时代，干出了一片新天地。

浙江义乌城西街道五一村，一幢幢白墙黑瓦的新中式联排房时尚典雅，让人误以为走进了城市里的别墅区。义乌先行先试开展农村宅基地所有权、资格权、使用权"三权分置"改革，在确保"户有所居"前提下，改革更进一步，实现宅基地资格权权益跨村调剂。试点以来，改革赋予农民更多财产权利，激

活农村沉睡资产 100 亿元，为农村发展提供了新动能。

当前全球经济复苏曲折前行的背景之下，哪个国家的营商环境好，那里的投资吸引力就强，那里的经营主体活力就高，这个国家经济的内生增长动力和韧性就好。中国大力推进"放管服"改革，营造公平竞争的市场环境，让国企敢干、民企敢闯、外企敢投……新冠疫情期间，各地针对市场经营主体出台各项纾困解难举措，帮助行业企业渡过难关，"青山常在、生机盎然"。

中国在世界银行《营商环境报告》中的排名从 2018 年的第 78 位升至 2020 年的第 31 位，跃升了近 50 位，连续两年成为全球优化营商环境改善幅度最大的十大经济体之一。

改革开放只有进行时，没有完成时。走到新的历史十字路口，中国内外环境都在发生极为广泛而深刻的变化，改革进入"深水区"，难免遇到难啃的"硬骨头"。未来，实现中国式现代化必然要坚定不移地全面深化改革开放。其中一个重要方面就是坚持社会主义市场经济改革方向，充分发挥社会主义市场经济的体制优势，推动有效市场和有为政府更好结合。

（二）改革是有方向、有立场、有原则的

当前中国正在将全面深化改革实践不断推向深入，但全面深化改革不意味着全都改，中国的改革是有方向、有立场、有原则的，该改的、能改的坚决改，不该改的、不能改的坚决不改。

社会主义方向是中国改革的根本方向。改革最根本的立场

就是人民立场。中国改革中最旗帜鲜明的一条原则就是坚持中国共产党的领导。中国共产党领导是中国特色社会主义最本质的特征，是中国特色社会主义制度的最大优势。这些都是必须坚持、决不能改的。

中国的改革是在坚持和发展社会主义制度的前提下，通过调整生产关系与生产力、上层建筑与经济基础不适应的部分和环节，协调"有形的手"与"无形的手"，使中国特色社会主义制度不断完善、生产力不断发展。

中国通过创新市场活动监管方式，深入推进公平竞争政策实施，加强反垄断和反不正当竞争。例如面对治理垄断资本等全球性难题，中国在发挥资本作为生产要素积极作用的前提基础上，完善法律制度体系，依法加强有效监管，为其设置"红绿灯"，防止资本脱实向虚、野蛮生长，更好地发挥资本在推动生产力发展、社会财富创造、民生保障和改善等方面的重要作用。

（三）以高水平开放促改革、促发展

对外开放是推动中国经济社会发展的重要动力，以开放促改革、促发展是中国发展不断取得新成就的重要法宝。

改革开放后，中国敞开大门，在顺应世界发展潮流中，抓住经济全球化战略机遇，加入世界贸易组织，在自身努力和全球发展中迎来了经济腾飞。

新时代以来，中国坚定不移扩大对外开放，实行更加积极主动的开放战略，构建面向全球的高标准自由贸易区网络，形成了更大范围、更宽领域、更深层次对外开放格局。

"尽管存在挑战，美国公司和中国公司仍表现出极大的韧性。"美中贸易全国委员会会长克雷格·艾伦带来一组数据：2022年美国和中国货物贸易总额创历史新高；美对华出口支撑了美国近百万个就业岗位。[①]中国欧盟商会调查则显示，超六成受访欧盟企业认为中国是其前三大投资目的地之一。中国欧盟商会主席伍德克表示，欧盟在华企业的选择，充分体现了对开放的中国市场充满信心，"希望成为中国发展故事的一部分"。

面向未来，"中国开放的大门只会越来越大"。

进一步完善知识产权法律保护体系，建立健全数字经济背景下知识产权保护的法律法规；出台外商投资法及其实施条例，实施准入前国民待遇加负面清单管理制度，外商投资准入负面清单持续"瘦身"……

中国坚定不移推进高水平对外开放，持续由商品和要素流动型开放向规则、规制、管理、标准等制度型开放拓展；坚持经济全球化正确方向，推动贸易和投资自由化便利化，在开放中不断增强中国式现代化建设的动力和活力，也不断以中国新发展为世界提供新机遇。

[①]《引擎·信心·机遇——全球财经大咖共话中国经济发展前景》，新华社，2023年3月26日。

五、加快发展新质生产力

高质量发展是全面建设社会主义现代化国家的首要任务，发展新质生产力是推动高质量发展的内在要求和重要着力点。新质生产力是创新起主导作用，摆脱传统经济增长方式、生产力发展路径，具有高科技、高效能、高质量特征，符合新发展理念的先进生产力质态。它由技术革命性突破、生产要素创新性配置、产业深度转型升级而催生，以劳动者、劳动资料、劳动对象及其优化组合的跃升为基本内涵，以全要素生产率大幅提升为核心标志，特点是创新，关键在质优，本质是先进生产力。[1] 加快发展新质生产力，是抢占新一轮全球科技革命和产业变革制高点、开辟发展新领域新赛道、培育发展新动能、增强竞争新优势的战略选择。

（一）科技创新是核心要素

科技创新能够催生新产业、新模式、新动能，是发展新质生产力的核心要素。发展新质生产力必须加强科技创新特别是原创性、颠覆性科技创新，加快实现高水平科技自立自强，壮大战略性新兴产业、积极发展未来产业。

---

[1]《习近平在中共中央政治局第十一次集体学习时强调 加快发展新质生产力 扎实推进高质量发展》，新华社，2024年2月1日。

中国式现代化发展之路

根据世界知识产权组织（WIPO）发布的《2023年全球创新指数》，中国是前30名中唯一的中等收入经济体，排名第十二位，在全球五大科技集群中占据三席。2023年，全社会研究与试验发展（R&D）经费支出3.3万亿元，与GDP之比达2.64%；[①] 企业创新主体地位进一步强化，中国高新技术企业数量从2012年的4.9万家增加至约40万家，增长达8倍，拥有的全球百强科技创新集群数量已跃居世界第一。

天津市滨海新区国家超级计算天津中心，一个"超强大脑"正日夜不息地运转。作为中国第一台千万亿次超级计算机，数十万台普通笔记本电脑同时计算，才能赶上它的速度。

从首次发布火星全球影像图，到每秒实现百亿亿次计算的超级计算机，中国不断加强原创性、引领性科技攻关，推动自主创新屡创新高。近年来，中国不断加强基础研究和原始创新，破解"卡脖子"难题，一些关键核心技术实现突破。

从"神舟飞天"到"蛟龙入海"，从"嫦娥揽月"到"天问探火"，从"北斗指路"到"墨子传信"……大国重器见证着中国攀登世界科技高峰的步伐。

中国式现代化关键在科技现代化，加快发展新质生产力为中国式现代化和高质量发展提供了坚实的物质技术基础。

[①] 国家统计局：《中华人民共和国2023年国民经济和社会发展统计公报》，2024年2月29日。

（二）人才是第一资源

人才是形成新质生产力最活跃、最具决定意义的能动因素。中国正按照发展新质生产力要求，从畅通教育、科技、人才的良性循环，完善工作机制保障，加大人才培养力度，从收入分配激励等方面着力，进一步培厚人才成长土壤，营造鼓励创新、宽容失败的良好氛围，让创新人才的"关键变量"转化为加快形成新质生产力的"最大增量"。

在山东青岛，一台激光雷达设备通过三维扫描，可以将万米范围内的风场信息变成可视化数据，不仅能观测风，还能预测风。这项技术20多年前就在中国海洋大学产生，曾为北京冬奥会、珠峰科考提供气象保障，却没有及时走出实验室。近年来，山东优化资源要素配置，支持企业联合高校、科研院所开展技术攻关，为科研人员匹配市场开发团队，推动试验技术产品与应用场景融合，引入天使投资，按照市场逻辑去分析判断科研成果，推动科研成果走向市场应用。如今，测风激光雷达已赋能千行百业。短短五年时间，青岛镭测创芯科技有限公司的年产值已突破1亿元，年均增长率达到70%。[①]

中国研发人员全时当量由2012年的324.7万人年提高到2022年的635.4万人年，稳居世界首位；顶尖科技人才国际学

---

① 《"新""新"向荣强动能——山东加快培育新质生产力观察》，新华社，2024年1月28日。

术影响力持续提升，入选世界高被引科学家数量从 2014 年的 111 人次增至 2022 年的 1169 人次，排名世界第二。①

（三）因地制宜发展新质生产力

中国幅员辽阔、人口众多，各地资源禀赋和发展水平千差万别。中国发展新质生产力不是忽视、放弃传统产业，而是各地立足实际，有选择地推动新产业、新模式、新动能发展，用新技术改造提升传统产业，积极促进产业高端化、智能化、绿色化。

机械手臂在空中有序地舞动着，切边剪裁、质量检查、张贴标签……走进包头钢铁（集团）有限责任公司的稀土钢冷轧板材厂，偌大的厂房内几乎见不到人，但所有设备都在按部就班地工作，一个自动化、智能化、信息化的工厂映入眼帘。尽管近些年钢铁行业下行压力较大，但靠着地方政策支持和自身全面转型，包钢集团不仅扭亏为盈，更是借助新能源快速发展的新机遇，找到了转型新风口。

为加快形成新质生产力，贵州积极推动各行业应用场景向华为云开放，目前选择了酱酒、煤矿、化工、有色金属、电力、新材料、钢铁、建材八大产业以及城镇智慧化改造、乡村数字化建设、旅游场景化创新、政务便捷化服务四大领域，深耕华为云盘古大模型在重点行业场景应用。

---

① 《我国研发人员全时当量达 635.4 万人年》，新华社，2023 年 12 月 15 日。

六、作为系统工程推进

中国式现代化是全面的现代化,涉及经济、政治、文化、社会、生态文明各个领域,关系改革发展稳定、内政外交国防、治党治国治军等方方面面,是一个社会整体跃升的变革过程。相应地,推进中国式现代化也由诸多领域、诸多环节、诸多层面构成,需要统筹兼顾、系统谋划、整体推进。

(一)在系统谋划中推进中国式现代化

推进中国式现代化是一场广泛而深刻的社会变革,往往牵一发而动全身,需要做好宏观的系统谋划。

中共二十大报告把中国式现代化置于新时代新征程中国共产党中心任务的战略高度进行顶层设计,不仅对全面建成社会主义现代化强国作出了战略安排,明确了各阶段的奋斗目标以及实现目标的时间表和路线图,而且从加快构建新发展格局、实施科教兴国战略、发展全过程人民民主、坚持全面依法治国、推进国家安全体系和能力现代化等12个方面对各领域各方面工作作出了系统谋划和科学部署。

推进中国式现代化,是一项前无古人的开创性事业,许多事情无前例可循,许多未知领域需要逐步挺进,许多事业需要在摸索中前进、在实践中成长、在创新中推动。中国共产党在推动事业发展中一直注重处理好顶层设计与实践探索关系,既发挥顶层设计的引领、规划和指导作用，也不断解放思想、大胆探索，摸着石头过河，支持和鼓励基层进行试点试验，如支持上海浦东新区打造社会主义现代化建设引领区，支持浙江高质量发展建设共同富裕示范区，福建、江西、贵州、海南设立了国家生态文明试验区等，在顶层设计与实践探索的协同联动中推动中国式现代化行稳致远。

（二）在统筹兼顾中推进中国式现代化

中国式现代化的系统性、整体性、复杂性、艰巨性，决定了它在推进中需要统筹兼顾，处理好一些重大关系。

——统筹效率与公平。一方面持续提升经济实力、释放社会活力，实现了比资本主义更高的效率，创造了经济快速发展的奇迹；一方面有效维护社会公平，坚持以人民为中心的发展思想，强调全体人民共同富裕，统筹城乡平衡和区域平衡，让每个人都有机会参与现代化进程、享受现代化红利。

——统筹改革、发展和稳定。一方面提升发展活力，抓住人民最关心的利益问题全面深化改革，发展全过程人民民主，广泛凝聚社会共识，创新基层社会治理，充分调动人民的积极性、主动性、创造性；一方面促进秩序安定，把握社会可承受程度来决定改革力度和发展速度，实现了发展活力和安定秩序有机统一，创造了社会长期稳定的奇迹。

——统筹发展与安全。一方面始终保持积极姿态，注重把握重大历史和战略机遇，加入世界贸易组织融入经济全球化浪潮，积极布局新一轮科技革命和产业变革；一方面坚持防范和化解重大风险，健全国家安全体系，确保重要产业链供应链安全，准备应对随时可能发生的各种"黑天鹅""灰犀牛"事件。

（三）整体推进中国式现代化

中国式现代化是经济、政治、文化、社会、生态文明"五位一体"的全面现代化，它们不是简单的并列关系，而是相辅相成、高度耦合的有机整体，指望单点爆破、单兵突进是不可能实现的，只有整体推进才能全面向前发展。

具体到经济、政治、文化等每一个领域的现代化，同样需要整体推进。在现代化进程中，中国之所以仅用几十年时间就走完发达国家200多年走过的工业化历程，就在于走的是一条不同于西方发达国家从工业化、城镇化向农业现代化、信息化顺序发展的"串联式"发展道路，而是工业化、信息化、城镇化、农业现代化叠加发展的"并联式"发展。

当然，整体推进也需要放远目光、放宽视野来看，它并非强调绝对的整齐划一，而是在各方面条件的基础上循序渐进、分步实施，讲究整体推进和重点突破，最终追求各方面全面进步，是一个接续奋斗、一代接着一代干的历史过程。以中国的改革开放为例，中国的改革是先从农村起步的，之后再过渡到城市，先从单一经济领域发展到其他各领域的；中国的开放是先从南方特别是东南沿海地区开始的，逐步向北方和中西部内陆扩展，开放的方位、层次和领域也是逐渐增加的。经过 40 余年，中国的改革开放仍在向纵深不断丰富和深入，这是中国式现代化整体推进的写照。

推进中国式现代化是一项充满艰辛和挑战的事业，异常复杂，会遇到各种可以预见和难以预见的困难。中国共产党对此有清醒的认识，始终坚持系统观念，用普遍联系的、全面系统的、发展变化的观点，把握好全局和局部、当前和长远、宏观和微观、主要矛盾和次要矛盾、特殊和一般的关系，不断提高辩证思维和底线思维，提高自身执政能力和领导水平，为系统推进中国式现代化源源不断注入动力。

第三章

中国式现代化的鲜明特色

　　一个国家走向现代化，既要遵循现代化一般规律，更要符合本国实际，具有本国特色。中国式现代化既有各国现代化的共同特征，更有基于自己国情的鲜明特色。[①]

——习近平

　　现代化是与工业化大生产方式相配套的，包括市场化、民主化、法治化、城镇化等多个方面发展内容的综合概念。工业革命以来，各国现代化都具有从传统向现代转变的共同特征，但也各具特色。

---

① 《习近平在学习贯彻党的二十大精神研讨班开班式上发表重要讲话强调 正确理解和大力推进中国式现代化 李强主持 赵乐际王沪宁蔡奇丁薛祥李希出席》，新华社，2023年2月7日。

事实证明，一个国家选择什么样的现代化道路，是由其历史传统、社会制度、发展条件、外部环境等诸多因素决定的。中国从自己的国情出发，走出了一条具有本国特色的现代化发展道路，创造了一个又一个世界瞩目的辉煌成就，向世界展现了中国式现代化的独特魅力。

一、人口规模巨大的现代化

人口基数大、城乡区域发展水平差异大是中国长期以来形成的基本国情。14亿多人口整体迈入现代化，规模超过现有发达国家人口的总和，这决定了中国式现代化是人类历史上规模最大、惠及人口最多的现代化，也是难度最大的现代化。

（一）惠及人口最多、最伟大的现代化

中国式现代化，在14亿多人口的发展中大国推进，其体量超过现有发达国家的人口总和，是人口规模巨大的现代化。第一次工业革命开始时，英国人口不到600万；第二次工业革命时期，美国人口不到8000万。到2019年，全世界已实现现代化的国家和地区的总人口还不到10亿。拥有14亿多人口的中国整体迈入现代化社会，将彻底改写现代化的世界版图。因此，

习近平指出："我们的现代化既是最难的，也是最伟大的。"①

中共十八大以来，中国共产党组织实施了人类历史上规模最大、力度最强的脱贫攻坚战，全面建成了人类有史以来惠及人口最多、规模体量最大的小康社会，不仅拓展了发展中国家走向现代化的途径，还为解决人类问题贡献了中国智慧和中国方案。清华大学当代国际关系研究院客座研究员、英国学者马丁·雅克认为，中国的人口规模、独立感和认同感、丰富的历史遗产以及卓越的政治领导力使它能够实现中国式的现代化道路，"我们现在正处于一个伟大的历史关头。现在，现代化不再是一小部分人的事，而是越来越多的人可能享受到的"，"西方的时代是少数人的时代，而未来的时代将是大多数人的时代"。②

（二）充足人力资源和超大规模市场积蓄发展潜力

改革开放以来，中国大量的农村剩余劳动力从农业向非农产业特别是制造业转移，释放出规模巨大的"人口红利"，推动城乡、区域以及产业之间资源重新配置。近10年来，中国在

---

① 《为全面建设社会主义现代化国家而团结奋斗——写在中国共产党第二十次全国代表大会胜利闭幕之际》，新华社，2022年10月23日。
② 《马丁·雅克：中国式现代化将惠及世界大多数人》，环球网，2023年5月12日，https://opinion.huanqiu.com/article/4CrBgxTvuxF。

加速制造业转型升级的同时，力促网络经济、平台经济等新业态发展，大量青年进入第三产业就业。2022年末，中国拥有近9亿劳动力。近年来，全国城镇新增就业平均每年超过1200万人。[①]中共十八大以来，中国通过实施就业优先战略，消除影响平等就业的不合理限制和就业歧视，使人人都有通过勤奋劳动实现自身发展的机会，居民人均可支配收入从2013年的18311元增加到2023年的39218元，消费水平不断提高。巨大的消费群体和强大的购买力持续推进消费转型升级，推动形成统一流通的超大规模市场，带动基建、交通、信息产业、服务业等巨大发展。充足的人力资源和超大规模的市场是推进中国式现代化的宝贵财富，为推动高质量发展积蓄强大动能。

中国互联网科技零售企业美团，为中国解决庞大人口就业问题提供了范本。作为中国最大的本地化科技零售企业，美团现有外卖、餐饮、酒店、旅行等超过200个生活服务场景，在国内服务930多万商户和6.8亿用户，不仅吸引大量人员就业，还带动数量庞大的骑手群体：2022年共有624万多名骑手通过美团获得收入，日均活跃骑手数量达100多万名；从2018年到2023年，美团平台上来自国家重点帮扶县的骑手从12万人增至约39.5万人，覆盖全部160个重点帮扶县。中国的互联网企业为数众多，淘宝、京东、拼多多、大众点评、携程等耳熟

[①]《新增1200万人以上，2024年如何稳住就业大盘？》，新华社，2024年3月5日。

能详的电商平台都与美团一样，不仅构建起规模巨大的网络市场，也成为吸纳人员就业的超大平台。

（三）开启世界历史上规模最大、速度最快的城镇化进程

城市是现代化的重要载体。改革开放前，中国城镇人口占比不到18%。改革开放以来，中国开启了世界历史上规模最大、速度最快的城镇化进程。如今，在上海、广东、江苏、浙江等东部不少地区，城市与农村已经融为一体；在西部大开发政策的持续推动和重庆、成都、西安等中心城市的辐射下，西部地区多个城市群蓬勃发展，城乡融合发展速度加快，城乡差距呈缩小趋势。数据显示，2023年末中国常住人口城镇化率已经达到66.16%。[1]2022年发布的"十四五"规划纲要提出，中国将坚持走中国特色新型城镇化道路，深入推进以人为核心的新型城镇化战略，以城市群、都市圈为依托促进大中小城市和小城镇协调联动、特色化发展，使更多人民群众享有更高品质的城市生活。

随着农村基础条件的改善和各类城乡融合政策的吸引，中国许多农村不再是生产力落后的代表，而是不少城市人才创业创新的舞台、向往的乐土。城市人才、资本、技术与乡村土地、

---

[1] 国家统计局：《中华人民共和国2023年国民经济和社会发展统计公报》，2024年2月29日。

劳动力等优势相结合，为传统农业转型注入了新元素、新能量，既满足了城市新需求、市民新诉求，也丰富了农业新业态。

（四）解决好巨量人口蕴藏的多样复杂诉求

任何一个小问题，如果乘以中国的 14 亿多人口，都会变得很大。中国庞大的人口基数背后，是各地区、各行业、各群体之间差异化的利益诉求和巨大的粮食、医疗、教育、养老、治安等民生保底需求，这给中国式现代化带来了很大挑战。中国把解决好百姓的急难愁盼问题当成改善民生的重中之重，始终保持历史耐心，坚持稳中求进、循序渐进、持续推进，将人口挑战转变为现代化发展的规模优势。

作为人多地少的国家，中国始终把粮食安全当成"国之大者"，近年来严格规范耕地占补平衡，稳妥有序落实耕地进出平衡，牢牢守住 18 亿亩耕地红线，确保端牢中国人自己的饭碗。目前中国已累计建成超 10 亿亩高标准农田，粮食生产实现"二十连丰"，总产量连续 9 年保持在 1.3 万亿斤以上；口粮自给率在 100% 以上，人均粮食占有量 490 公斤，高于国际公认的 400 公斤粮食安全线。[①]

在应对居民人身安全诉求问题上，中国已被国际社会公认

[①] 国家统计局：《中华人民共和国 2023 年国民经济和社会发展统计公报》，2024 年 2 月 29 日。

为世界上最安全的国家之一。中国一贯加强社会治安综合治理，纵深推进扫黑除恶，刑事立案总量、主要刑事案件和查处治安案件数量连年下降。如今，每当夜幕降临，中国各个城市的居民都会无忧无虑地在街巷和公园里散步、健身、游乐。在中国知名视频App"哔哩哔哩"上，一位外国青年表示："人们常常会忽略中国的闪光点，因为他们对中国没有宽容的心态，自己又不愿意来体验。安全就是中国的闪光点之一。"

二、全体人民共同富裕的现代化

共同富裕是中国特色社会主义的本质要求，是中国共产党人始终不渝的奋斗目标。中国式现代化致力于让发展成果更多更公平惠及全体人民，不断满足人民日益增长的美好生活需要，推进共同富裕，防止两极分化，实现社会和谐稳定、经济持续发展。

（一）"一个也不能掉队"

从老子"损有余而补不足"到孔子"不患寡而患不均"，从管仲的"凡治国之道，必先富民"到《礼记·礼运》描绘的"大同"社会……纵观中华民族五千多年文明史，共同富裕的理想深深植根于中华优秀传统文化中。

继承弘扬中华优秀传统文化的中国共产党，把实现全体人民共同富裕作为重要奋斗目标，坚持发展为了人民、发展依靠人民、发展成果由人民共享。毛泽东提出，"这个富，是共同的富，这个强，是共同的强，大家都有份"；邓小平强调，"让一部分人、一部分地区先富起来，大原则是共同富裕"；习近平指出，"我们说的共同富裕是全体人民共同富裕，是人民群众物质生活和精神生活都富裕，不是少数人的富裕，也不是整齐划一的平均主义"。对于来自人民、代表人民、始终致力于为人民服务的中国共产党来说，共同富裕既是长远目标，更是现实行动。

中国不仅历史性解决了绝对贫困问题、全面建成小康社会，而且通过推进中国式现代化建设，不断提高全体人民的生活水平。目前，中国中等收入群体超过4亿人，居民人均可支配收入超3.9万元，[1]实现从低收入国家到中等偏上收入国家的历史性跨越。

一个试点，一组数据，生动展示共同富裕"中国样本"：2023年，浙江高质量发展建设共同富裕示范区，居民人均可支配收入达到6.38万元，[2]城乡居民收入比从2012年的2.37下降到2023年的1.86。

---

[1] 国家统计局：《中华人民共和国2023年国民经济和社会发展统计公报》，2024年2月29日。
[2] 浙江省统计局：《2023年浙江省人民生活等相关统计数据公报》，2024年3月4日。

（二）织就全球最大社会保障网

民生是共同富裕的重要表现和基本内容。中国式现代化坚持尽力而为、量力而行，在就业、教育、社保、医疗等方面向农村、基层、欠发达地区倾斜，向困难群众倾斜，夯实共同富裕的兜底保障。

当前，中国已建成世界上规模最大的教育体系、社会保障体系、医疗卫生体系。2023年统计数据显示：九年义务教育巩固率、高中阶段毛入学率分别达到95.7%和91.8%；基本养老保险覆盖近11亿人，医保参保人数超过13亿人，有4400万人被纳入低保和特困救助范围；共有医疗卫生机构107.1万个，全年总诊疗人次达95.6亿人次。[1]

为缩小区域差距，近年来，中国中央财政持续加大对地方转移支付力度，重点向困难地区和欠发达地区倾斜，优先保障教育、医疗等领域普惠性、基础性、兜底性民生支出。2023年中央对地方转移支付10.29万亿元，规模为历年来最大。[2]

（三）把"蛋糕"做大做好，切好分好

在中国式现代化进程中，共同富裕不是空泛的政治宣誓，

---

[1] 国家统计局：《中华人民共和国2023年国民经济和社会发展统计公报》，2024年2月29日。
[2] 财政部：《2023年中国财政政策执行情况报告》，2024年3月7日。

而是一个政党团结带领全体人民进行的一场伟大社会变革：有效市场和有为政府一齐发力，全国人民共同奋斗把"蛋糕"做大做好，然后通过合理的制度安排把"蛋糕"切好分好。

分配制度是促进共同富裕的基础性制度。中国统筹效率和公平，构建初次分配、再分配、三次分配协调配套的基础性制度安排。中国不断提高劳动报酬在初次分配中的比重，实现居民收入增长和经济增长基本同步、劳动报酬提高和劳动生产率提高基本同步。各地因地制宜不断提高最低工资标准，增加劳动者特别是一线劳动者劳动报酬。完善按要素分配政策制度，多措并举促进农民增收，有效保障农民工工资发放。中国不断完善再分配机制，加大调节力度和精准性。个人所得税起征点从改革开放之初的每月800元提高到目前的每月5000元，并增加子女教育支出、大病医疗支出、住房贷款利息和住房租金等专项附加扣除，让每个人的钱包更加充实。中国还注重发挥第三次分配的作用，发展慈善事业，倡导企业家积极参与和兴办社会公益慈善事业，做到富而有责、富而有义、富而有爱。

共同富裕是长远目标，贯穿中国式现代化全过程，不可能一蹴而就。中国坚信，只要坚持推动高质量发展，切实解决发展不平衡不充分的问题、持续缩小城乡区域发展差距，坚持发展成果让全体人民共享，共同富裕就一定会实现。

三、物质文明和精神文明相协调的现代化

中国式现代化既要物质富足，也要精神富有，始终坚持物质文明与精神文明相互协调、相互促进。没有先进文化的积极引领，没有人民精神世界的极大丰富，没有民族精神力量的不断增强，一个国家、一个民族不可能屹立于世界民族之林。

（一）繁荣文化事业和文化产业

中国式现代化注重健全现代公共文化服务体系，创新实施文化惠民工程，提高基本公共文化服务的覆盖面和适用性，切实保障人民群众基本文化权益。中国通过推广优秀的电影、电视剧、戏剧、广播剧、图书等文艺作品，不断丰富改造人们的精神世界。中国免费开放公立博物馆、图书馆、美术馆、文化馆站等，将全民阅读上升为国家发展战略。当前，中国共有3300多家公共图书馆[①]、10万余家实体书店、58.7万家农家书屋，播种下一颗颗阅读的种子，构建起涵育文明风尚的精神家园。

（二）提高全社会文明程度

核心价值观是一个民族赖以维系的精神纽带，是一个国家

---

① 国家统计局：《中华人民共和国 2023 年国民经济和社会发展统计公报》，2024 年 2 月 29 日。

共同的思想道德基础。中国式现代化致力于弘扬富强、民主、文明、和谐，自由、平等、公正、法治，爱国、敬业、诚信、友善的社会主义核心价值观，巩固团结奋斗的思想基础、培育开拓进取的主动精神、弘扬健康向上的价值追求。

立德树人——中国建立健全党和国家功勋荣誉表彰制度，挖掘传播典型人物践行社会主义核心价值观的先进事迹，引导全社会学习效仿。近年来，中国评选出一批时代楷模、全国道德模范、诚信之星、"新时代好少年"，这些"最美中国人"用高尚人格点亮人类的道德天空，激励一代代中国人向上向善，永远奋斗。在先进人物的引领下，见义勇为、拾金不昧、尊老爱幼、乐于助人等凡人善举在中国社会不断涌现，引导人们树立并践行正确的世界观、人生观、价值观。

以文化人——中国式现代化注重用社会主义先进文化、革命文化、中华优秀传统文化培根铸魂，在中华优秀传统文化的创造性转化和创新性发展中建设社会主义精神文明。近年来，中国深入推进中华文明探源工程、中华文化资源普查工程，"唐宫夜宴""典籍里的中国"等一大批创新产品带动文博热。中国还成为图书、电视剧、动漫等领域世界第一生产大国，电影市场规模屡创纪录，银幕数和票房收入跃居全球第一，《敢教日月换新天》《长津湖》《觉醒年代》等一批重点作品脱颖而出，实现从"高原"向"高峰"的迈进。

系统育人——中国式现代化构建"文明城市、文明村镇、文明单位、文明家庭、文明校园"精神文明创建体系，全面推进新时代文明实践中心建设，深入开展群众性精神文明创建活动，推动社会主义核心价值观融入社会发展各方面，转化为人们的情感认同和行为习惯。志愿服务是社会文明进步的重要标志。中国注册志愿者人数从 2012 年的 292 万人增长到 2023 年的 2.32 亿人，[①]2022 年至 2023 年社区志愿服务累计总时长达 15.69 亿小时。在湖南衡阳，近 150 万群众成为注册志愿者，每 5 人中就有 1 人加入"衡阳群众"志愿服务队，哪里有需要，他们就出现在哪里，充分展现了中国特色志愿服务事业焕发出的勃勃生机。

人民有信仰，国家有力量，民族有希望。中国式现代化之所以能闯关破障、行稳致远，根本原因在于中国共产党团结带领全国各族人民，凝聚最大合力、步伐一致向前进。

（三）提高国家文化软实力

中国式现代化吸收借鉴和创造性应用一切人类优秀文明成果，把马克思主义基本原理同中国具体实际相结合、同中华优秀传统文化相结合，坚持创造性转化、创新性发展，大力发展社会主义先进文化，以全方位的社会进步彰显现代化的系统性

---

① 中国社会科学院社会发展战略研究院、中国志愿服务研究中心：《志愿服务蓝皮书：中国志愿服务发展报告（2022～2023）》，社会科学文献出版社 2024 年版。

协调性。

中国始终注重保护好、传承好本国文化遗产，做好考古成果的挖掘、整理、阐释工作，注重开发文化和文化遗产的多重价值。"国家宝藏""中国考古大会"等文化节目获得高收视率和高讨论热度，激发广大群众的文化自信。中国努力构建有中国特色、中国风格、中国气派的哲学社会科学学科体系、学术体系、话语体系。中国文艺工作者扎根人民、扎根生活，积极创造出一大批表现当代中国人民奋斗历程和生活状态的优秀作品，一些作品在海外也广受欢迎。

四、人与自然和谐共生的现代化

绿色是中国式现代化的鲜明底色。中国坚持可持续发展，统筹推进经济社会发展和生态环境保护，坚持节约优先、保护优先、自然恢复为主的方针，坚定不移走生产发展、生活富裕、生态良好的文明发展道路，实现中华民族永续发展。历史与现实一再警示，大自然是人类赖以生存发展的基本条件，只有遵循自然规律才能有效防止在开发利用自然上走弯路。中国式现代化倡导尊重自然、顺应自然、保护自然，践行"绿水青山就是金山银山"的理念，促进人与自然和谐共生。

（一）"绿水青山就是金山银山"

"绿水青山就是金山银山"，这是重要的发展理念，也是中国推进现代化建设的重大原则，揭示了保护生态环境就是保护生产力、改善生态环境就是发展生产力的道理。良好的生态环境是最公平的公共产品，也是最普惠的民生福祉，这已成为中国全社会的思想共识和行动自觉。

近年来，中国政府以解决损害群众健康的突出环境问题为重点，深入打好蓝天、碧水、净土保卫战。例如，长江流域的地方各级政府对长江"共抓大保护、不搞大开发"，长江干流水质近年来一直稳定保持在Ⅱ类，这项环保工作覆盖中国11个省市，惠及全国40%以上的人口。

中国将生态功能极重要、生态极脆弱以及具有潜在重要生态价值的区域划入生态保护红线，实现一条红线管控重要生态空间，中国陆域生态保护红线面积占陆域国土面积比例超过30%。2023年，中国地级及以上城市优良天数比率为86.8%，重污染天数比率下降到1.1%，成为全球大气质量改善速度最快的国家。作为长江上游最大江心岛，重庆广阳岛按照"共抓大保护、不搞大开发"的思路停止开发地产、开展生态修复。如今，岛上草长莺飞、溪流潺潺，成为游人向往的"长江风景眼、重庆生态岛"。

（二）统筹山水林田湖草沙一体化保护和系统治理

中国贯彻绿色发展理念，划定并严守生态保护红线、环境质量底线和资源利用上线，努力构建以国家公园为主体、自然保护区为基础、各类自然公园为补充的自然保护地体系，加强生物多样性保护。截至目前，已正式设立三江源、大熊猫、东北虎豹、海南热带雨林、武夷山首批5个国家公园，建立各级各类自然保护地近万处，90%的陆地自然生态系统类型、65%的高等植物群落、74%的国家重点保护野生动植物物种得到有效保护，300余种珍稀濒危野生动植物种群得到恢复性增长，初步建立起新型自然保护地体系。在云南，流域面积2920平方公里的滇池是中国西南地区最大湖泊，[①] 历经数十年坚持不懈大投入、大治理，水质从劣Ⅴ类变为Ⅳ类，局部水域达到Ⅲ类。

（三）推动形成绿色发展方式和生活方式

中国协同推进降碳、减污、扩绿、增长，探索一条生态优先、节约集约、绿色低碳的人与自然和谐共生的现代化新路径。

斗转星移，气象更新。云南大理拆除洱海临湖客栈民宿、建设生态廊道，鞍钢矿业曾经尘土飞扬的矿山蜕变为绿色生态

[①] 昆明市水务局：《昆明市水务局关于对政协昆明市十四届一次会议第141370号提案的答复》，2022年5月30日，https://shuiwu.km.gov.cn/c/2022-05-30/4603910.shtml。

园……2023年全国两会期间，一组卫星对比图在海外社交媒体刷屏。从卫星视角俯瞰中国，中华大地上的沧桑巨变，生动诠释着中国式现代化的生机与活力。惊叹于过去10年中国的发展成就，海外网友纷纷留言，"这是真正的变化""很令人钦佩"。

绿色发展离不开绿色能源。中国深入推进能源革命，加强煤炭清洁高效利用，加快规划建设新型能源体系。沙漠里，成千上万块光伏板逐日追光；海面上，大风车耸立于碧海蓝天间化风为电；长江干流上的6座巨型梯级水电站"连珠成串"，构成世界最大"清洁能源走廊"。2023年，天然气、水电、核电、风电、太阳能发电等清洁能源消费量占能源消费总量比重上升至26.4%。[①]

中国式现代化致力于推动产业结构、能源结构、交通运输结构等调整优化，加快形成绿色低碳的生产方式和生活方式，以高品质的生态环境支撑高质量发展。作为一个负责任大国，中国秉持"人与自然是生命共同体"的理念，作出了2030年前实现碳达峰、2060年前实现碳中和的重要承诺，将立足自身能源资源禀赋，力争用全球历史上最短时间实现碳达峰到碳中和。

---

① 国家统计局：《中华人民共和国2023年国民经济和社会发展统计公报》，2024年2月29日。

（四）超越人类中心主义自然观，强调人与自然是生命共同体

近代以来，西方现代化以资本为中心追求利益最大化，将自然界视为人类获取物质财富的载体，导致严重的环境危机，带来严峻的环境问题。随着西方国家向发展中国家复制西方现代化模式并向发展中国家转嫁其产业成本，这种以牺牲生态环境为代价推进的现代化，也蔓延到全球南方国家，全球性生态环境问题愈演愈烈。

中国式现代化，坚持人与自然和谐共生，超越了西方现代化将人凌驾于自然之上的人类中心主义自然观。这一独特的生态观，植根于中华优秀传统文化"天人合一""道法自然""取之有度、用之有节"等思想，强调人与自然是生命共同体，坚持节约优先、保护优先、自然恢复为主的方针，尊重自然、顺应自然、保护自然，像保护眼睛一样保护生态环境，像对待生命一样对待生态环境，还自然以宁静、和谐、美丽。

中国式现代化通过科学统筹自然系统和人类社会各方面要素，探索出一条发展与保护协同并进的新路径，同时，也为共谋全球生态文明建设、推动构建地球生命共同体贡献智慧和力量。

五、走和平发展道路的现代化

立足世界百年未有之大变局，胸怀中华民族伟大复兴战略全局，中国共产党人高举和平、发展、合作、共赢的旗帜，弘

扬全人类共同价值，倡导并推动构建人类命运共同体，坚定地走依靠和平发展实现现代化的道路。

（一）在坚定维护世界和平与发展中谋求自身发展

中华民族经历了西方列强侵略、凌辱的悲惨历史，深知和平的宝贵。中国式现代化不走殖民掠夺的老路，不走国强必霸的歪路，始终坚持把现代化建立在和平发展的基础上，坚定维护以联合国为核心的国际体系、以国际法为基础的国际秩序、以联合国宪章宗旨和原则为基础的国际关系基本准则，主张以团结精神和共赢思维应对复杂交织的安全挑战，致力构建公道正义、共建共享的安全格局。中国是全球唯一将"坚持和平发展道路"载入宪法的国家，是派遣维和人员最多的联合国安理会常任理事国，也是核武器大国中唯一承诺不首先使用核武器的国家。中国共产党着眼于人类未来命运，开辟了一条强而不霸的现代化发展之路。

在湖南衡阳、山东泰安等中国多地，自古以来就建有儒、释、道三教合一的寺庙并保存至今，儒家的"仁义礼智信"思想、佛教的慈悲善行等观点、道教的"道法自然""大道无为"等理念，在中国不仅没有产生冲突和对抗，反而和谐共生、美美与共，构成了中华文明多元一体的显著特性。

本着这一特性，中国始终倡导讲信修睦、亲仁善邻，把人类命运共同体理念与协和万邦的邦交之道相融通，以"海纳百川、有容乃大"阐述全球事务应由各国共同治理，以"和羹之美，在于合异"倡导多样性的人类文明应该交流互鉴、共同进步，以"大道不孤、天下一家"倡导世界各国携手并进、共建美好地球家园。因此，中国人不认同"零和博弈"，而是把"和则两利、斗则两伤"作为普遍认知和行为准则。

中华民族的血液中没有侵略他人、称王称霸的基因。在"和合文化"的影响下，中国在2000多年前就开通了丝绸之路，促进了沿线国家和地区的融合发展。600多年前，明朝航海家郑和率领当时世界上最强大的船队多次乘风破浪南下太平洋、印度洋，足迹遍布亚洲、非洲的30多个国家和地区，不仅从未侵占一寸土地，而且一路播撒和平和友谊的种子。

当前，中国不断推动世界贸易组织、亚太经合组织等多边机制更好发挥作用，扩大二十国集团（G20）、金砖国家、上海合作组织等多边合作机制影响力，增强新兴市场国家和发展中国家在全球事务中的代表性和发言权。为缓和沙特和伊朗两国紧张关系，中国成功斡旋并促成双方恢复建立外交关系，有力维护中东地区和平稳定。面对乌克兰危机，中国秉持客观中立的立场，根据事情本身的是非曲直决定自己的立场和政策，坚持劝和促谈。

（二）以自身发展更好维护世界和平与发展

中国式现代化是向全世界敞开大门的现代化。中国坚定走互利共赢的全球化发展道路，积极参与全球治理体系建设和改革、践行真正的多边主义，推动贸易自由化、投资便利化，促进国际宏观经济政策协调，营造有利于各国共同发展的国际环境，培育全球发展新动能，致力于缩小南北差距，帮助发展中国家加快发展。

2013年，中国先后提出建设"丝绸之路经济带"和"21世纪海上丝绸之路"的合作倡议。据2023年10月发布的《共建"一带一路"：构建人类命运共同体的重大实践》白皮书显示，十年来，中国秉承共商共建共享的原则，已与150多个国家、30多个国际组织签署了200多份共建"一带一路"合作文件，形成一大批标志性项目和惠民生的"小而美"项目。中国连续举办六届中国国际进口博览会、十届中国国际服务贸易交易会、三届中国国际消费品博览会，与世界共享中国市场、中国机遇。

2022年1月1日，中国等15国共同签署的《区域全面经济伙伴关系协定》（RCEP）正式生效实施，全球人口最多、经贸规模最大、最具发展潜力的自贸区启航。在逆全球化思潮抬头、世界经济复苏乏力背景下，RCEP政策红利不断释放，成为世界经济增长的最大亮点。2023年，中国对RCEP其他14个成员国合计进出口额约12.6万亿元，较协定生效前的2021年增长5.3%。[①] 联合国贸易和发展会议秘书长蕾韦卡·格

[①] 国务院：《国务院新闻办就2023年全年进出口情况举行发布会》，2024年1月12日。

林斯潘表示，在全球开放程度不断下降、贸易成本不断上升、供应链出现瓶颈的情况下，RCEP为世界经济发展作出贡献。在促进全球开放合作与维护多边贸易体制方面，中国发挥着越来越重要的作用。

中国共产党认为，任何国家追求现代化，都应该秉持团结合作、共同发展的理念，走共建共享共赢之路。正如习近平所说："走在前面的国家应该真心帮助其他国家发展。吹灭别人的灯，并不会让自己更加光明；阻挡别人的路，也不会让自己行得更远。"

第四章

中国式现代化创造人类文明新形态

中国式现代化，深深植根于中华优秀传统文化，体现科学社会主义的先进本质，借鉴吸收一切人类优秀文明成果，代表人类文明进步的发展方向，展现了不同于西方现代化模式的新图景，是一种全新的人类文明形态。[1]

——习近平

文明指人类社会进步的状态，不是从来就有，也不是一成不变，而是在生产力发展的推动下逐步演进升级、生长传播的。现代文明是迄今为止人类社会进步所取得的最高成果，带来了

---

[1]《习近平在学习贯彻党的二十大精神研讨班开班式上发表重要讲话强调 正确理解和大力推进中国式现代化 李强主持 赵乐际王沪宁蔡奇丁薛祥李希出席》，新华社，2023年2月7日。

翻天覆地的"古今之变"，但并不意味着人类文明已到达美好的终点。

　　社会制度是文明发展的产物，也是文明变化升华的基础。资本主义制度所创造的生产力，虽然"比过去一切世代创造的全部生产力还要多，还要大"①，但并没有解决好人类社会发展的诸多难题。当今世界，多重挑战和危机交织叠加，发展鸿沟不断拉大，人类社会现代化进程又一次来到历史的十字路口。

　　为彻底改变中华民族历史命运，抱着对人类更好社会制度探索的使命，中国共产党带领中国人民，经过百年奋斗，成功走出了中国式现代化道路，创造了人类文明新形态。随着理论不断完善，实践不断深化，这种中国特色社会主义的文明形态充分展现出全新现代文明的鲜明特色、显著优势和全球影响力。

一、新价值形态：追求人民至上

　　价值观是文明的灵魂，决定文明的演进历程与最终走向。中国式现代化与西方式现代化在价值取向上的本质区别在于：摒弃资本至上，追求人民至上。

　　资本至上是资本主义文明的基本价值理念。西方式现代化

---

① ［德］卡尔·马克思、弗里德里希·恩格斯著，陈望道译：《共产党宣言》，湖南人民出版社 2021 年版。

以资本为中心，由资本驱动，也被资本裹挟，其带来生产力的快速发展和物质的极大丰裕，改善了人们的生活，但也造成物质主义膨胀、贫富两极分化等无法避免的恶果。

中国式现代化把实现人民对美好生活的向往作为现代化建设的出发点和落脚点，以实现人的自由而全面的发展为最终目标，在价值形态上对西方式现代化实现了"原点超越"。

（一）以实现人民对美好生活的向往为实践起点

"人民对美好生活的向往，就是我们的奋斗目标。"2012年11月15日，在北京人民大会堂面对中外记者，新当选的中国共产党中央委员会总书记习近平用一句生动、凝练的话语，对中国共产党坚持人民至上的执政理念和价值追求作了最好诠释。

中国式现代化不是为了现代化而现代化，而是为了不断增进人民福祉。中国始终牢牢把握现代化的"人民性"方向，更好回应人民各方面诉求和多层次需要，不仅要看纸面上的指标数据，更要看人民的幸福安康，由此避免了西方现代化进程中的方向偏离和路径依赖。

（二）以实现人的自由而全面的发展为最终目标

在中国式现代化的价值形态中，现代化的本质是人的现代化，而不是物的现代化；是人的全面现代化，而不是人的片面现代化。

中国式现代化把提高人口整体素质同人民高品质生活紧密结合起来,一方面加快塑造素质优良、总量充裕、结构优化、分布合理的现代化人力资源,以人口高质量发展支撑中国式现代化;另一方面,推动物质文明和精神文明协调发展,在中华大地上实现高楼大厦与精神大厦的辉映并立。

(三)以发展成果惠及全体人民为检验标准

实现全体人民共同富裕的现代化,是中国式现代化的本质要求之一。

与西方贫富两极分化的现代化不同,中国式现代化追求的不仅是富裕,而是全体人民共同富裕;不是一部分人的现代化,而是全体人民的现代化。从打赢脱贫攻坚战到全面推进乡村振兴,从建设共同富裕示范区到深化东西部协作和定点帮扶……中国通过有效举措,努力让现代化建设成果更多更公平惠及全体人民。

中国在推进现代化进程中,打赢脱贫攻坚战,使中国从一穷二白、积贫积弱的东方大国实现了彻底告别绝对贫困,使占世界五分之一人口的大国摆脱绝对贫困,创造了人类社会发展史上绝无仅有的巨大成就。中国成为世界第二大经济体,国内生产总值突破百万亿元大关,人均国内生产总值超过一万美元,改变了中华民族近代以后在世界经济体系中的边缘性地位和落后处境,而且以自身发展对世界经济作出巨大贡献,极大提升了广大发展中国家的经济地位。

中国作为人口规模巨大的发展中大国实现现代化，将极大改变世界现代化版图，成为世界百年未有之大变局中极大的积极变化。长期以来，西欧国家、美国以及一些深受欧美西方文化影响的资本主义国家被看作现代和先进的代表，发展中国家则被看作传统和落后的代表。一些西方国家建立起先天的优越感，形成了凌驾于非西方国家和民族之上的霸权意识，西方中心主义盛行。中国式现代化的巨大成功强烈冲击了西方国家的优越感和傲慢，极大提升了广大发展中国家的国际地位、话语权和影响力。

二、新制度形态：不断完善革新

上世纪90年代，苏联解体、东欧剧变，世界社会主义运动遭遇重大挫折，"历史终结论"一时甚嚣尘上，西方发达资本主义国家的社会制度被定义为"人类意识形态发展的终点"[1]和"人类最后一种统治形式"[2]。进入二十一世纪，随着社会主义中国的快速崛起，科学社会主义焕发出勃勃生机。中国式现代

---

[1] [美]弗朗西斯·福山著，陈高华译：《历史的终结与最后的人》，广西师范大学出版社2016年版。
[2] 同上。

化与西方现代化在制度建设上的高下之分在于：证伪"历史终结论"，不断完善革新。

（一）拥有核心领导力量的制度

新中国成立70多年来，中华民族之所以能迎来从站起来、富起来到强起来的伟大飞跃，最根本的是因为中国共产党领导人民建立和完善了中国特色社会主义制度。

"读懂今天的中国，必须读懂中国共产党。"中国特色社会主义最本质的特征是中国共产党领导，中国特色社会主义制度的最大优势是中国共产党领导，中国共产党的领导制度是中国的根本领导制度。

在推进中国式现代化进程中，中国共产党不断深化对共产党执政规律、社会主义建设规律、人类社会发展规律的认识；坚持自我革命，把自身建设和国家现代化建设紧密结合起来，始终奋发有为，确保现代化领导的坚定性和持续性。中国共产党领导的多党合作和政治协商制度被称为"新型政党制度"，能够实现利益代表的广泛性，体现奋斗目标的一致性，促进决策施策的科学性，保障国家治理的有效性，有效避免出现党派纷争、利益集团偏私、少数政治"精英"操弄等现象。

（二）有科学理论指导的制度

中国特色社会主义制度是以马克思主义为指导、植根中国大地、具有深厚中华文化根基、深得人民拥护的制度。马克思主义具有鲜明的实践品格，不仅致力于科学"解释世界"，而且致力于积极"改变世界"。

一百多年来，中国共产党从初心使命出发，不断进行理论创新，不断推进马克思主义基本原理同中国具体实际、同中华优秀传统文化相结合，从而始终保持生机活力。从毛泽东思想、邓小平理论、"三个代表"重要思想、科学发展观，到习近平新时代中国特色社会主义思想，中国共产党坚持"两个结合"，不断推进马克思主义中国化时代化，为现代化建设提供行动指南。

围绕"什么是中国式现代化、怎样推进中国式现代化"这条主线，中国共产党人创造并不断续写走社会主义道路成功建设现代化的奇迹，形成了内容丰富的中国式现代化理论，对中国式现代化的中心任务、科学内涵、中国特色、本质要求、战略安排、总体目标、主要目标任务、重大原则等进行全面阐发，升华了对既往现代化实践经验的理解，实现了对社会主义现代化理论的原创性发展。

（三）不断吸收人类文明成果的制度

中国不照搬照抄他国政治制度模式，但也不排斥任何有利于本国发展进步的他国国家治理经验。在社会主义建设时期，中国的国家制度和国家治理体系就借鉴吸收了苏联的许多有益经验。改革开放以来，中国不断扩大对外开放，把社会主义制度和市场经济有机结合起来。

改革开放之初，中国国内也存在社会主义和市场经济对立的思想教条。中国以调整生产关系为主要改革内容，通过经济运行机制和所有制结构变革，建立起公有制为主体、多种所有制经济共同发展的创新型经济结构，推动各种所有制取长补短、相互促进、共同发展，既发挥了市场经济的长处，又发挥了社会主义制度的优越性，解答了这个世界经济史上"最难的加法"。中共十八大以来，中国继续在社会主义制度与市场经济的有机结合上下功夫，把两方面优势都发挥好，既要"有效的市场"，也要"有为的政府"，极大解放和发展了社会生产力，极大增强了社会活力。

三、新发展形态：走向全面协调

文明是人类在认识世界和改造世界中创造的有形和无形的积极成果的总和。追求进步是文明的生长逻辑，全面协调是文明发展的内在要求。中国式现代化与西方现代化在路径选择上的显著差别在于：走出"单向""异化"，走向全面协调。

（一）锚定"人的现代化"起步探索

在大文明观下，物质文明是始终处于主导地位的、最基础的文明，但在资本逻辑主导下，对物质财富的"单向"追求不仅造成了一系列社会问题，还加剧了人的"异化"，现代文明给人类带来了很多，也让人失去了很多。

1964年，美国学者马尔库塞出版《单向度的人》一书，提出美国这样的发达工业社会不是真正自由开放的社会，而是"单向度"的社会，它用无尽的消费和享受来贿赂大众，让人们陷入"舒适的不自由"之中。经过深入研究，马尔库塞对现代资本主义社会提出更加尖锐的批评：发达的资本主义社会虽然变得更富裕了，但人的"异化"不仅没有消失，反而更深入、更广泛，也更隐秘地渗透到生活的所有领域，无论是经济、政治还是文化都被商品拜物教所支配，生活在这种社会中的人是丧失了真正自由的"单面人"。

而中国式现代化从起步之时，就锚定"人的现代化"，探索全面协调发展之路。

（二）全面协调发展布局逐步成型

物质贫困不是社会主义，精神贫乏也不是社会主义。从"两个文明"到"五个文明"，中国全面协调发展布局逐步成型。

早在1982年，中国共产党第十二次代表大会就首次从战略高度提出"在建设高度物质文明的同时，一定要努力建设高度的社会主义精神文明"的现代化发展目标。2012年，党的十八大确立了经济建设、政治建设、文化建设、社会建设、生态文明建设"五位一体"的总体布局,坚持经济建设是根本,政治建设是保障,文化建设是灵魂,社会建设是条件,生态文明建设是基础,促进了物质文明、政治文明、精神文明、社会文明、生态文明的有机协同,推动中国式现代化协调发展。经过十年实践,硕果累累,谱写了人类文明史册的新华章,宣示着人类文明迎来新发展阶段。

(三)在着力破解不平衡不充分矛盾中统筹推进

2017年,中共十九大报告明确提出:进入新时代,中国社会主要矛盾已经转化为人民日益增长的美好生活需要和不平衡不充分的发展之间的矛盾。面对这一关系全局的历史性变化,中国共产党贯彻以人民为中心的发展思想,以更好满足人民在经济、政治、文化、社会、生态等方面日益增长的需要为导向,大力提升发展质量和效益,着力解决发展不平衡不充分问题。

物质文明建设成效显著,政治文明建设稳步推进,精神文明建设精彩纷呈,社会文明建设创新发展,生态文明建设日新月异,新时代十年中国交出了全面协调发展的新答卷。

现代化是一个复杂的系统,其发展程度越高,系统特征越显著,对整体协同的要求越高。正是在"五位一体"总体布局的引领下,中国人民美好生活需要被全方位多层次动态认识和把握,人民最关心最直接最现实的利益问题被关注并不断解决,人民获得感、幸福感、安全感更加充实、有保障、可持续。

四、新民主形态：全过程人民民主

民主是多数人享有国家权利的政治制度，它的实质是人民当家作主，在现代社会中是一种有效治理手段。然而在国际上，民主这个词已被西方"注册"，导致国际舆论场上民主叙事以西方为主。在多数西方人眼中，民主模式就是西方的多党制和普选制，但在中国人眼中，这只是西方民主的一种形式。中国式现代化与西方式现代化在治理机制上最大不同在于：超越形式民主，推进全过程人民民主。

（一）民主是用来解决问题的

放眼全球，在一些自称民主"世界样板"的国家，国家治理"失灵""低效"，社会撕裂严重；在一些"复制粘贴"西方民主模式的发展中国家，出现了"有民主、无治理"的悖反现象。

随着时间的推移，衡量民主的西方中心主义标尺已经过时。人们逐渐开始以民主的治理效能替代民主的程序优先作为对民主效能的评判标准。民主不是装饰品，不是用来做摆设的，而是要用来解决人民的问题的。

在中国共产党的逻辑里，人民当家作主的"实质性民主"是价值逻辑，而发展"全过程民主"，让老百姓能够享受和平发展的红利、过上安宁祥和的幸福生活则是效用逻辑。

（二）广泛、真实、管用的民主

坚持中国共产党的领导、人民当家作主、依法治国有机统一是中国人民民主制度的核心。坚持中国共产党的领导回答了"谁来凝聚人民"，坚持人民当家作主回答了"民主的目标为何"，坚持依法治国回答了"如何治理国家"。

其内在机理是：人民通过中国共产党领导凝聚为有机整体；党和人民共同意志体现并成为宪法和法律；国家以宪法为根本法得以组织、运行和发展；权力运行必须在法治的框架内；人民以中国共产党为核心，通过各种途径和形式依法管理国家事务、管理经济和文化事业、管理社会事务，宪法、法律及其实施都要有效体现人民意志、保障人民权益、激发人民创造力。

（三）打破"唯选票"模式保障人民权利

全过程人民民主是中国民主的基本特征，是指国家机器运转的每一个环节都必须体现民主，而不仅限于投票环节。这种民主打破了"唯选票"的模式，保障了人民的民主选举、民主协商、民主决策、民主管理、民主监督等权利，涵盖国家生活和社会生活的方方面面。

瑞士伯尔尼艺术大学名誉教授贝亚特·施耐德观察到，他所熟悉的中国民主制度，有各级民主机构和人民代表大会，中国共产党不仅亲民，更是与人民团结在一起，与西方国家每四年一次的选举相比，这是一个优势。

哈佛大学肯尼迪政府学院2020年发布的《理解中国共产党韧性：中国民意长期调查》报告显示，2003年以来，中国民众对政府的满意度不断提升，对中国共产党的满意度超过90%。[1] 从国家政策的影响到地方官员的行为，中国民众认为政府比以往任何时候都更有能力、更有效率。

（四）广泛凝聚共识，提升治理效能

全过程人民民主之所以"最管用"，是因为这种民主的精神、制度与机制，有效渗透到中国政治体系和治理实践之中。全过程人民民主集中体现了人民总体意志，是主体最广泛的民主，广泛汇集人民群众的意见表达；不断丰富完善的民主协商制度，是"找到全社会意愿和要求的最大公约数"的有效途径；如此基于广泛参与主体的共识，为有效治理提供了动力。

全过程人民民主存在于民主的全链条，全流程机制弥补治理缝隙，全过程品质奠定整体性治理；坚持全过程人民民主，更好地服务于人民群众的公共利益，以人民群众的力量和智慧为依托，使国家治理更好地体现人民意志、保障人民权益，是提升国家治理效能的关键。

---

[1] "Understanding CCP Resilience: Surveying Chinese Public Opinion Through Time"，July, 2020, https://ash.harvard.edu/publications/understanding-ccp-resilience-surveying-chinese-public-opinion-through-time.

五、新文化形态：坚持继承创新

文化是民族的血脉，是人民的精神家园。文化自信是一个国家、一个民族发展中最基本、最深沉、最持久的力量。优秀传统文化中深藏着时代价值，经过创造性转化、创新性发展，释放出与当代文化相适应、与现代社会相协调的巨大能量。中国式现代化与西方式现代化在文化认同上鲜明差异是：从不割裂传统，坚持继承创新。

（一）守护文化根脉，传承文明薪火

中华优秀传统文化源远流长、博大精深，是中华文明的智慧结晶和精华所在，是中华民族的根和魂，是中国在世界文化激荡中站稳脚跟的根基。中国式现代化秉持大历史观，从历史长河、时代大潮、全球风云中分析演变机理、探究历史规律，提出因应的战略策略。

西方经典现代化理论一些观点认为，传统与现代相互对立、相互排斥，传统必然阻碍现代化，推进现代化必然要否定、抛弃传统。还有一些观点否定不同国家历史进程的差异性，认为世界各国推进现代化的进程是对西方式现代化模式的不断重复。

中国在探索现代化道路上，长于从贯通古今中外的视角审视人类社会现代化发展历史，尊重历史规律和文化传统，把握现在，开创未来，体现出中华民族五千多年文明积淀的深厚历史底蕴。

中国是世界四大文明古国之一，中华文明是其中唯一传承至今未曾中断的文明。中华文明探源工程等重大工程的研究成果，实证了中国百万年的人类史、一万年的文化史、五千多年的文明史。已故著名华裔考古人类学家张光直提出"连续性"与"破裂性"理论，他认为以中国为代表的"连续性"宇宙观和文明发展道路，不同于西方文明的"破裂性"宇宙观和文明发展道路，为我们重新审视人类文明发展的一般规律提供了不同以往的视角。

世界历史发展证明，一个国家选择什么样的现代化道路，既应遵循现代化一般规律，更要符合本国实际，根据其历史传统、社会制度、发展条件、外部环境等诸多条件作出选择。中国认为总结历史经验、把握历史规律，才能掌握现代化发展的历史主动，从而抓住历史变革时机，顺势而为，奋发有为，更好前进。

（二）创造性转化、创新性发展

中华优秀传统文化中，孕育着国家治理的思想智慧，对解决人类社会共同难题有着深刻的思想启示。在现代化进程中，中国推动中华优秀传统文化创造性转化、创新性发展，深入挖掘和阐发中华优秀传统文化中天下为公、民为邦本、为政以德、革故鼎新、任人唯贤、天人合一、自强不息、厚德载物、讲信修睦、亲仁善邻等的时代价值，使中华优秀传统文化成为涵养社会主义核心价值观的重要源泉，不断把马克思主义思想精髓同中华优秀传统文化精华贯通起来。

中国推进马克思主义中国化时代化，推进"两个结合"，推动中华优秀传统文化的创造性转化和创新性发展，建构马克思主义基本原理同中华优秀传统文化相结合的新的文化生命体。在这一过程中，马克思主义基本原理同中华优秀传统文化彼此契合、相互成就，经由"结合"，形成了中国式现代化的新的文化形态，造就了一个有机统一的新的文化生命体，即中华民族现代文明。

（三）平等共存，交流互鉴

文明因交流而多彩，文明因互鉴而丰富。文明差异不应该成为世界冲突的根源，而应该成为人类文明进步的动力。中国式现代化秉持平等、互鉴、对话、包容的文明观，以文明交流超越文明隔阂、以文明互鉴超越文明冲突、以文明包容超越文明优越，为世界文明朝着平衡、积极、向善的方向发展提供助力。西方现代化理论认为，人类社会发展划分为"文明"与"野蛮"两大阶段，世界划分为"现代工业社会"和"非工业社会"，西方"现代工业社会"是整个非西方世界的榜样，西方文明是人类文明的顶峰。

中国人认为，人类只有肤色语言之别，文明只有姹紫嫣红之别，但绝无高低优劣之分，人类社会创造的各种文明为各国现代化积蓄了厚重底蕴。中国式现代化倡导尊重世界文明多样性，秉持平等和尊重，摒弃傲慢和偏见，加深对自身文明和其他文明差异性的认知,不同文明和谐共生。各种文明本没有冲突,我们既要让本国文明充满勃勃生机,又要为他国文明发展创造条件,让世界文明百花园群芳竞艳。

中华文明自古就以开放包容闻名于世,在同其他文明的交流互鉴中不断焕发新的生命力。中国式现代化,深深植根于中华优秀传统文化,深入挖掘和阐发中华优秀传统文化的时代价值和中华文明的精神特质,体现科学社会主义的先进本质,借鉴吸收一切人类优秀文明成果,代表人类文明进步的发展方向,展现了不同于西方现代化模式的新图景。中国式现代化作为人类文明新形态,与全球其他文明相互借鉴,必将极大丰富世界文明百花园,为解决人类社会共同难题提供思想启示,为人类现代化发展提供精神指引。

六、新全球治理形态:构建人类命运共同体

和平如阳光,安全似雨露,受益而不觉,失之则难存。面对风云变幻的时代、动荡变革的世界,各国人民对和平安宁的期盼愈加强烈。中国发展现代化,既造福中国人民、又促进世界共同发展,在推进强国建设和民族复兴的同时,谋求人类进步和世界大同。中国式现代化与西方式现代化在全球治理认知格局上差异在于:反对单边主义、保护主义,推动构建人类命运共同体。

（一）追求共同价值，守护共同命运

一个和平发展的世界应该承载不同形态的文明，必须兼容走向现代化的多样道路。中国大力弘扬和平、发展、公平、正义、民主、自由的全人类共同价值，摒弃小圈子和"零和博弈"，呼吁共同构建相互尊重、公平正义、合作共赢的新型国际关系，扩大利益汇合点，画出最大同心圆。

历史上，一些西方国家奉行对抗性"零和博弈"思维，凭借其现代化先发优势，向其他国家输出现代化模式，通过经济剥削、殖民掠夺等方式将本国财富积累的代价和危机转嫁至发展中国家，并且为现代化后发国家的经济和社会发展设置重重阻碍，导致世界现代化发展出现严重的不平衡、不公正问题。

中国秉承协和万邦的天下观，始终关注人类前途命运，努力以中国式现代化新成就为世界发展提供新机遇，坚持走和平发展的人间正道，倡导以对话弥合分歧、以合作化解争端，始终把自身命运同各国人民的命运紧密联系在一起，推动构建人类命运共同体。

中华民族传承和追求的是和平、和睦、和谐的理念。中国过去没有，今后也不会侵略、欺负他人，不会称王称霸。中国始终是世界和平的建设者、全球发展的贡献者、国际秩序的维护者、公共产品的提供者，将继续以中国的新发展为世界提供新机遇。

（二）维护共同秩序，完善全球治理

世界上既不存在定于一尊的现代化模式，也不存在放之四海而皆准的现代化标准。中国没有走一些国家通过战争、殖民、掠夺等方式实现现代化的老路。中国更反对个别国家恶意歪曲国际法含义，将自己的意志包装成所谓"基于规则的国际秩序"，强加于国际社会，大肆侵犯别国合法权利。

中国主张共商共建共享的全球治理观，积极参与、推动，并和各国一道，携手推进全球治理体系改革和建设，推动国际秩序朝着更加公正合理的方向发展，在不断促进权利公平、机会公平、规则公平的努力中推进人类社会现代化。

中国式现代化旨在破解现代化发展史中出现的、而西方国家并没有解决的诸多难题，比如以资本为中心而导致贫富两极分化、物质主义膨胀、对外扩张掠夺等。中国始终坚定站在历史正确的一边、站在人类文明进步的一边，高举和平、发展、合作、共赢旗帜，在坚定维护世界和平与发展中谋求自身发展，又以自身发展更好维护世界和平与发展。

（三）倡导共同行动，践行大国担当

2021年9月，中国提出全球发展倡议，主张以人民为中心、普惠包容、创新驱动、人与自然和谐共生等。中国认为，各国发展紧密相连，人类命运休戚与共，各国必须和衷共济，团结合作。

· 中国式现代化发展之路 ·

从 2021 年 9 月提出全球发展倡议，到 2022 年 4 月提出全球安全倡议，再到 2023 年 3 月提出全球文明倡议，习近平始终饱含对人类前途命运的深切关怀、对人类文明前景的深邃思索，为国际社会提供重要公共产品。三大倡议相继提出，不断丰富和拓展构建人类命运共同体的思想内涵和实践路径。在美国库恩基金会主席罗伯特·劳伦斯·库恩看来，人类命运共同体是"改善全球治理的伟大构想"，"这表明中国愿为促进世界和平与繁荣承担更多全球责任"。①

中国式现代化拓展了发展中国家走向现代化的途径，为广大发展中国家提供了全新选择，为人类对更好社会制度的探索提供了中国方案。每个国家自主探索符合本国国情的现代化道路的努力都应该受到尊重，发展中国家有权利也有能力基于自身国情自主探索各具特色的现代化之路。中国将始终坚持把国家和民族发展放在自己力量的基点上，把国家发展进步的命运牢牢掌握在自己手中，尊重和支持各国人民对发展道路的自主选择，共同绘就百花齐放的人类社会现代化新图景。

---

① 《为解决人类面临的共同问题作出贡献——国际社会眼中的中共二十大》，新华社，2022 年 10 月 27 日。

结　语

当前，世界之变、时代之变、历史之变正以前所未有的方式展开。新一轮科技革命和产业变革深入发展，和平赤字、发展赤字、安全赤字、治理赤字加剧。世界进入新的动荡变革期，又一次站在历史的十字路口，何去何从取决于各国人民的抉择。

如果说西方现代化是人类现代化的序曲，那么包括中国在内的发展中国家则越来越多地融入了人类现代化的交响。

人类追求现代化的历史，是一部不同文明在交流互鉴中推陈出新的历史。在追求现代化的艰苦卓绝奋斗中，中国共产党领导中国人民成功走出了中国式现代化道路，创造了人类文明新形态，拓展了发展中国家走向现代化的途径，为人类对更好社会制度的探索提供了中国方案。

中国式现代化，是中国共产党领导的社会主义现代化。善于守正创新的中国共产党,把马克思主义基本原理同中国具体实际相结合、同中华优秀传统文化相结合,不断推进马克思主义中国化时代化。在此基础上,中国式现代化又以生动实践和巨大成果丰富了科学社会主义理论,把追求共同富裕变成实际行动,让天下大同等理想不再遥不可及。

推进中国式现代化,也是一项开创性事业,必然会遇到各种可以预料和难以预料的风险挑战、艰难险阻甚至惊涛骇浪。我们应当清醒地看到,当今世界,霸权主义、强权政治、霸凌行径对世界和平造成严重冲击,一些国家鼓噪分裂对抗,大搞"脱钩断链",给全球安全带来巨大威胁;地区安全热点问题此起彼伏,局部冲突和动荡频发,传统和非传统安全威胁交织叠加;逆全球化思潮抬头,保护主义明显上升,世界经济复苏乏力……

前途光明,任重道远。中国共产党人从来不会躺在自己的功劳簿上沾沾自喜,也不会屈服于外界的压力而裹足不前。同时,中国共产党人坚持走和平发展的现代化道路,坚信人类是一个有机整体,地球是一个共有家园。面对共同挑战,任何人、任何国家都无法独善其身,人类只有和衷共济、和合共生这一条出路。中华民族历来讲求"天下一家",主张民胞物与、协和万邦、天下大同,憧憬"大道之行,天下为公"的美好世界,致力于推动构建人类命运共同体。

万物并育而不相害,道并行而不相悖。只有各国行天下之大道,和睦相处、合作共赢,繁荣才能持久,安全才有保障。

结 语

中国坚持对话协商，推动建设一个持久和平的世界；坚持共建共享，推动建设一个普遍安全的世界；坚持合作共赢，推动建设一个共同繁荣的世界；坚持交流互鉴，推动建设一个开放包容的世界；坚持绿色低碳，推动建设一个清洁美丽的世界。

中国相信，全世界只要携起手来，坚持和平发展、合作共赢，坚持弘扬平等、互鉴、对话、包容的文明观，弘扬全人类共同价值，就一定能够共创现代化的美好未来，共创人类文明的美好明天。

· 中国式现代化发展之路 ·

编写说明与致谢

　　《中国式现代化发展之路》智库报告课题组由中央党史和文献研究院院长、中央党史和文献研究院国家高端智库理事会理事长曲青山和新华通讯社社长、新华社国家高端智库学术委员会主任傅华任组长，新华通讯社总编辑吕岩松任副组长，新华通讯社副总编辑任卫东与中央党史和文献研究院学术和编审委员会主任（副部长级）王均伟任执行副组长，中央党史和文献研究院课题组成员包括张鹏、李琦、刘敏茹、范为、郑林华、董晓彤、周思勤、曲世侠、桑田等，新华通讯社课题组成员包括刘刚、崔峰、林嵬、王金涛、杨守勇、傅琰、伍晓阳、郭强、凌军辉、毛振华、张紫赟、肖思思、杨皓、屈凌燕、周蕊、李放、蔡国栋、杜白羽、侯伟利、孙晓辉、马昌豹、刘爱虹、何慧媛、梁劲、冯候等。

课题自2023年1月立项启动以来，历时一年多采访、调研、撰写、修改、审校完成。

在报告写作和发布过程中，中央党史和文献研究院副院长季正聚、原中央党校副校长李君如、中国人民大学党委书记张东刚、中央党史和文献研究院第一研究部副主任樊锐、中央党史和文献研究院第一研究部一级巡视员张贺福、中央党史和文献研究院机关党委原副书记张爱茹、中国人民大学哲学院院长臧峰宇、中国社会科学院欧洲研究所副所长刘作奎、中国社会科学院美国研究所原副所长李文、北京大学国际关系学院教授潘维、中央党校（国家行政学院）文史教研部中国史教研室主任王学斌、新华社对外部中国国际传播研究中心副主任郭信峰等专家学者给予了多方面的帮助和指导，在此一并表示诚挚谢意。

Chinese Modernization:
The Way Forward

Introduction

With the Spinning Jenny kicking off the Industrial Revolution in the mid-18th century, Western countries started their journey to modernization.

Today, after more than 250 years, the tide of modernization is still surging forward. China, once languishing in untold suffering and turmoil, is now embarking on a glorious and promising new journey toward modernization under the leadership of the Communist Party of China (CPC).

Chinese modernization is socialist modernization pursued under the leadership of the CPC. It shares features common to the modernization processes of all other countries, but it is more characterized by features that are unique to the Chinese context. It is the modernization of a huge population, of common prosperity for all, of the coordinated pursuit of material and cultural-ethical advancement, of harmonious coexistence between humanity and nature, and of peaceful development.

Is there only one model of modernization in the world? Is there only one set of standards of modernization that applies to all countries? Based on an analysis of Chinese modernization's theory and practice, the answer is no.

This report reviews and analyzes the CPC's century-long dedicated efforts of leading the Chinese people in exploring a path to modernization. Since the founding of the People's Republic of China, and particularly since the CPC's 18th National Congress, China has made tremendous achievements lauded by the world in science and technology, economic development, ecological advancement, and many other fields.

This report outlines practical approaches to Chinese modernization. Under the leadership of the CPC, China will firmly adhere to a people-centered development philosophy, follow its own path, advance reform and opening up as a crucial move, develop new quality productive forces at a faster pace, achieve greater self-reliance and strength in science and technology, and advance modernization in all respects in a systematic way. Under the leadership of the CPC, the largest Marxist governing party in the world, China will be a pioneer in exploring green, low-carbon, and high-quality development, strive to build a human community with a shared future, and respond with composure and solid action to global changes of a magnitude unseen in a century.

Based on an in-depth analysis, this report asserts that Chinese modernization has given rise to a new form of human advancement. Chinese modernization is different from Western modernization in the following ways: it puts people, not capital, first; it debunks the idea of "the end of history" and pursues the constant improvement and innovation of systems and institutions; it pursues a model of comprehensive and coordinated development, not one-dimensionality and alienation; it ensures that the people run their country and that democracy is not practiced for the few; it strives to both preserve cultural heritage and enrich it; and it rejects unilateralism in global governance and advances the building of a human community with a shared future.

This report notes that modernization is not only about the economy, it is also about the well-rounded development of the people. Chinese modernization has set an example for developing countries to independently pursue a path to modernization. Its theory and practice offer a viable alternative for countries and nations that seek to develop themselves both rapidly and independently and give inspiration, hope, and confidence to other developing countries as they explore a path to modernization suitable to their national conditions.

The road ahead may be long and arduous, but with sustained efforts, we will reach our destination. The sun rising in the east will light up the road ahead.

Chapter One

The Evolution of Chinese Modernization

Since the very day of its founding, the Communist Party of China has made seeking happiness for the Chinese people and rejuvenation for the Chinese nation its aspiration and mission. All the struggle, sacrifice, and creation through which the Party has united and led the Chinese people over the past hundred years has been tied together by one ultimate theme—bringing about the great rejuvenation of the Chinese nation.[①]

—Xi Jinping

In 1921, on a boat at Nanhu Lake in Jiaxing, the first CPC National Congress was concluded, launching China on its hundred-year journey of modernization.

---

① Xi Jinping's speech at the ceremony marking the centenary of the Communist Party of China, Xinhua News Agency, July 1, 2021.

Chapter One The Evolution of Chinese Modernization

The founding of the CPC, inconspicuous in its beginnings, was a silent clap of thunder that marked the beginning of glorious and epic endeavors. From a Shikumen house on Xingye Road in Shanghai to Tian'anmen in Beijing, all the efforts, struggles and sacrifices the Party has made over one hundred years have been for the happiness of the people and national rejuvenation. Generation after generation of Chinese Communists have led the Chinese people in exploring and pursuing a path to modernization, scoring remarkable achievements along the way and making outstanding contributions to human advancement.

1. Achievements on a Hundred-Year Journey

Over the course of human progress, the Chinese nation has created an enduring and splendid civilization, long ranked among the great nations of the world, and made indelible contributions to the advancement of human civilization. After the mid-17th century, bourgeois revolutions erupted in a series of Western countries, which soon entered the Industrial Revolution. Driven by new models of production, they quickly grew in strength. The bourgeoisie of these countries, through blood and fire, started its early accumulation of capital and colonial plundering.

China, a country with vast territories, abundant resources, and a large population, however, gradually fell behind other countries in the global wave of advancement, industrialization, and modernization. As a result, it became a market coveted and fought over by Western powers. Starting in 1840, Western powers repeatedly invaded China and compelled it to cede territory and pay indemnities, grabbing all sorts of privileges. They thus gravely set back China's economic development and modernization process.

"Our country endured intense humiliation, our people groaned in misery, and our civilization was plunged into darkness[①]."—This observation fully captures what happened to China when it was dragged into a West-dominated wave of modernization. Countless dedicated patriots made every effort to learn advanced systems and technologies from Western countries, hoping to move China along a path to strength and prosperity. Undeterred by setbacks, they explored all possible ways to save China. A group of Qing government officials represented by Zeng Guofan, Li Hongzhang, Zuo Zongtang and Zhang Zhidong called for drawing from the techniques of Western countries; scholars like Kang Youwei and Liang Qichao advocated reform; and Sun Yat-sen and Huang Xing believed that the solution lied in revolution. However, despite their unyielding efforts, their plans ended in failure, and they failed to lift the old China out of weakness and poverty.

With the salvoes of Russia's October Revolution in 1917, Marxism-Leninism was introduced to China. From then on, Chinese Communists have shouldered the historic task of realizing China's modernization. Led by generation after generation of Chinese Communists, the Chinese people have ushered in a great transformation from standing up to growing prosperous and strong. By embarking on a Chinese path to modernization, China has made a historic transition from being dragged into Western modernization to leading the new wave of global modernization.

1) 1921-1949: Early explorations of modernization in the period of the new-democratic revolution

In 1921, when China was torn apart and bullied by foreign powers, the Communist Party of China was founded, and the Chinese people were granted the hope to free themselves from miseries and humiliations.

---

① Xi Jinping's speech at the ceremony marking the centenary of the Communist Party of China, Xinhua News Agency, July 1, 2021.

In exploring ways to save China, the early Chinese Communists soon realized that imperialism, feudalism, and bureaucrat-capitalism could not possibly give birth to new productive forces and that China first had to carry out a profound social revolution. China's modernization would be possible only with the independence of the Chinese nation and the liberation of the Chinese people.

During this period, the CPC rallied the Chinese people and led them in carrying out the new-democratic revolution, establishing a new China in which the people run the country and thus realizing China's independence and the people's liberation. This put an end to China's history as a semi-colonial, semi-feudal society, to the rule of a small number of exploiters over the working people, and to disunity that had plagued the old China. All the unequal treaties imposed on China by foreign powers and all the privileges they held in the country were abolished. China achieved a great transformation from a millennia-old feudal autocracy to a people's democracy. This created the fundamental social conditions for China to realize modernization.

2) 1949-1978: Explorations of modernization in the period of socialist revolution and construction

The founding of the People's Republic of China marked a historic turning point in China's transformation from a country in decline into a strong and prosperous one. This made it possible for China to build socialism and pursue modernization.

At its founding, the People's Republic was poor and weak, with a complete lack of heavy machinery manufacturing or other modern technology and equipment. As Mao Zedong pointed out, "What can we make at present? We can make tables and chairs, teacups and teapots, we can grow grain and grind it into flour, and we can make paper. But we can't make a single motor car, plane, tank, or tractor."

In December 1953, Mao Zedong proposed that China should develop "modernized industry," "modernized agriculture and transportation," and "modernized national defense." The proposition of "the four modernizations" thus began to take shape. In September 1954, on behalf of the CPC Central Committee, Zhou Enlai declared for the first time that China should develop modernized industry, agriculture, transportation, and national defense. At the First Session of the Third National People's Congress, held from the end of 1964 to the beginning of 1965, Zhou Enlai officially announced to the nation the strategic goal of achieving modernization of agriculture, industry, national defense, and science and technology.

To achieve the strategic goal of "the four modernizations," the CPC Central Committee put forward a two-step development plan in 1964. The first step was to establish an independent and relatively complete industrial system and national economic system. The second step was to fully realize the modernization of agriculture, industry, national defense, and science and technology so that China could rank among the world's leading economies.

Thanks to the dedicated efforts of the Chinese people, by the end of the 1970s, China had established an independent and relatively complete industrial system and economic system, accomplishing the first-step task of "the four modernizations" strategy. The creative theoretical achievements and great progress made in this period provided valuable experience, theoretical underpinnings, and material foundations for China's modernization.

3) 1978-2012: Advances in modernization in the new period of reform and opening up

In the late 1970s, as a new scientific and technological revolution unfolded, global modernization gathered pace. Facing new developments both at home and abroad, the CPC urgently needed to make political and strategic decisions regarding fundamental policies that would determine the future of the Party and the country.

At the Third Plenary Session of the 11th CPC Central Committee convened in December 1978, a historic decision was made to shift the priority of the

Party and the country's work agenda onto economic development and to launch reform and opening up. In March 1979, based on an assessment of the conditions in China, Deng Xiaoping creatively set the goal of achieving "Chinese-style modernization." In December of the same year, Deng Xiaoping used the term xiaokang (moderate prosperity), a distinctive term of traditional Chinese culture, to define Chinese modernization, setting forth well-defined parameters for the level of modernization China would achieve by the end of the 20th century. Xiaokang thus became a standard to be met in China's drive for modernization. In 1987, the CPC Central Committee adopted a three-step development strategy for achieving modernization. The first step was to meet the basic living needs of the Chinese people by the end of the 1980s. The second step was to achieve a moderately prosperous standard of living by the end of the 20th century. The third step was to generally achieve modernization and reach the level of a moderately developed country by the middle of the 21st century.

To advance China's modernization, Chinese Communists made bold explorations. They successfully integrated the socialist system with the market economy and made building a socialist market economy a goal of reform, thus ushering in a new stage of reform, opening up, and modernization. On December 11, 2001, China acceded to the World Trade Organization, becoming an integral part of globalization. This was a milestone in China's modernization drive. China aligned itself with WTO rules and promoted trade liberalization and investment facilitation. As it became more open, China added strong impetus to economic globalization and injected new vigor into world economy.

In this period, China achieved a historic transformation, changing from a country with a relatively low level of productivity to the world's second largest economy. It also made historic strides in raising the living standards of its people from bare subsistence to moderate prosperity on the whole, and then toward moderate prosperity in all respects. These achievements fueled China's modernization by providing new and dynamic systemic underpinnings and creating material conditions necessary for achieving rapid development.

4) 2012-present: Chinese modernization on all fronts in the new era

After the 18th National Congress of the CPC in November 2012, socialism with Chinese characteristics entered a new era, and Chinese modernization advanced on all fronts. By fully reviewing and drawing on the practices of China's modernization, the CPC Central Committee with Comrade Xi Jinping at its core has continued to advance the cause and enrich the theory of Chinese modernization, thus opening up new horizons for rejuvenating the Chinese nation with Chinese modernization.

In terms of theory, with a deeper understanding of the substance and essence of Chinese modernization, a sound summary of its distinctive Chinese features, fundamental goals, and underlying principles, and the establishment of a preliminary theoretical framework, the concept of Chinese modernization has become better articulated and easier to understand and carry out. The new era is an irreversible historical process toward the rejuvenation of the Chinese nation. Against this backdrop, Xi Jinping Thought on Socialism with Chinese Characteristics for a New Era, rising to the occasion, represents a new breakthrough in adapting Marxism to the Chinese context and the needs of our times, and provides fundamental guidance for Chinese modernization.

In terms of strategy, a two-step strategy has been drawn up for building China into a great modern socialist country in all respects. The timeline is as follows: in the period from 2020 to 2035, generally achieve socialist modernization; in the period from 2035 to the middle of the century, develop China into a great modern socialist country that is prosperous, strong, democratic, culturally advanced, harmonious, and beautiful. To lay solid foundations for achieving modernization, steps have been taken to implement the Five-Sphere Integrated Plan to promote coordinated economic, political, cultural, social, and ecological advancement and the Four-Pronged Comprehensive Strategy to make comprehensive moves to build a modern socialist country, deepen reform, advance law-based governance, and strengthen the Party's self-governance.

In addition, a series of major strategies have also been developed, such as the strategy for invigorating China through science and education, the strategy on developing a quality workforce, and the rural revitalization strategy.

In terms of practice, the CPC Central Committee with Comrade Xi Jinping at its core has rallied the entire Party and Chinese people and led them in working tirelessly and making historic achievements and changes in the cause of the Party and the country in the new era. In particular, China has put an end to absolute poverty that had plagued it for thousands of years, accomplished the First Centenary Goal of building a moderately prosperous society in all respects on schedule, and created a miracle in the history of poverty reduction. These represent a solid step toward the goal of delivering prosperity for all.

Advancing Chinese modernization is an unprecedented and groundbreaking endeavor. In the new era, China has adopted transformative practices, made new breakthroughs, and scored landmark accomplishments. All of this has provided more solid systemic underpinnings, laid stronger material foundations, and created a reliable source of inspiration for pursuing Chinese modernization.

Thanks to ceaseless efforts made over the past century and more, China has opened new ground and achieved initial success in pursuing modernization. The theory and practice of Chinese modernization are based on China's specific conditions. They add new modern substance to Marxist theory on development, integrate and draw on fine traditional Chinese culture, and present a theoretical framework different from that of Western modernization. Chinese modernization has disproved the claim that "modernization equals westernization" and has enriched and developed the intellectual landscape of global modernization.

"The more daunting a task, the more admirable the efforts to accomplish it." On the new journey to continue the pursuit of Chinese modernization, the Communist Party of China will surely be able to rally the Chinese people and lead them in delivering a performance that stands up to the scrutiny of history .

2. Chinese Modernization Has Changed China

Under the leadership of the CPC, in just several decades, the Chinese people have completed the process of industrialization that took developed countries several centuries to complete. China has scored widely recognized achievements in modernization and realized two miracles—rapid economic growth and long-term social stability. It has grown from a country plagued by poverty and weakness into the world's second largest economy, achieving a historic leap in its composite national strength.

1) Eradicating absolute poverty and fulfilling the millennia-old dream of moderate prosperity in all respects

Achieving moderate prosperity is a dream long cherished by the Chinese nation. Since its 18th National Congress, the CPC has always prioritized poverty elimination in governance. Giving full play to the political strengths of its leadership and China's socialist system, the CPC adopted a wide range of distinctive and pioneering steps to launch the most far-reaching and intense drive to eliminate poverty in human history. Thanks to eight years of unremitting efforts, China met its goal of eliminating poverty on schedule. By the end of 2020, the 98.99 million rural residents living below the current poverty threshold, 832 poor counties, and 128,000 impoverished villages were all lifted out of poverty. Across the country, regional poverty was eradicated[1].

On July 1, 2021, at the ceremony marking the centenary of the CPC, Xi Jinping declared that, thanks to continued efforts of the whole Party and the entire nation, China has met the First Centenary Goal of building a moderately prosperous society in all respects, and the absolute poverty that had plagued the

---

[1] Xi Jinping's speech at a gathering marking the nation's poverty alleviation accomplishments and honoring model poverty fighters, Xinhua News Agency, February 25, 2021.

Chinese nation for thousand years has been eradicated once and for all, and we are now marching in confident strides toward the Second Centenary Goal of building China into a great modern socialist country in all respects. Realizing moderate prosperity in all respects represents the fulfillment of a key target on the way to modernization and national rejuvenation.

By reducing poverty, China has made an outstanding contribution to the world, accounting for over 70 percent of global poverty reduction, which marks a milestone in the development of human history[1]. China's targeted poverty alleviation efforts have broken new ground in the theory and practice of poverty alleviation and are highly relevant to other countries facing similar challenges. They demonstrate that human society has gone beyond what capitalism can do to eliminate poverty, thus turning a new page in humanity's pursuit of genuine equality.

2) Achieving rapid economic development and a historic leap in GDP

Since the CPC's 18th National Congress, China's economy has achieved a historic rise, with GDP growing from 53.9 trillion yuan in 2012 to 126 trillion yuan in 2023, or around US$18 trillion calculated at the average annual exchange rate. China is now the world's second largest economy and contributes more than 30 percent of global economic growth on average.

Quantitative and qualitative improvements in China's economy have driven global growth. Over the past decade, China has accelerated the transformation of its manufacturing industry from one that is only large in output to one that is advanced. Its service industry has become its largest sector, green development has become a core component, and consumption has become the primary engine

---

[1] "The achievements made by New China in its development over the past 70 years are of global and historic significance," Wang Zhidong, Guangming Daily, 6th page, October 16, 2019.

driving economic growth. China's urbanization rate has increased steadily, and food and energy security as well as living standards have been ensured. The value added of new sectors as well as new forms and new models of business now exceeds 17 percent of China's GDP. The share of China's GDP in the global economy between 2012 and 2021 rose from 11.4 percent to over 18 percent. In the last ten years, China's contribution to global economic growth has been larger than the combined total of the G7.

A high-standard open economy is taking shape. In recent years, China has continually cut tariffs, expanded market access, advanced opening up on a larger scale, across more areas, and in greater depth, and explored new ways of conducting foreign trade. Market access for foreign capital has been expanded further, and efforts have been accelerated to develop a high-standard open economy. China is becoming more open to the world, and this has greatly promoted global development and prosperity. China is now a major trading partner of more than 140 countries and regions and a main source of investment for a growing number of countries[①]. At a time when the global recovery lacks momentum, a steadily growing Chinese economy will bring much needed certainty to a world full of uncertainties and add vitality to global recovery.

3) With both vitality and order as well as development and stability, hundreds of millions of Chinese enjoy peace and prosperity

In the pursuit of rapid economic growth, the CPC has stayed committed to achieving prosperity for all. It endeavors to ensure both efficiency and fairness, both vitality and order, and both development and stability while striving to fulfill the Chinese people's wish for prosperity and peace. It has thus created a

---

[①] Building an open, inclusive and interconnected world for common development, keynote speech by Xi Jinping at the opening ceremony of the Third Belt and Road Forum for International Cooperation, Xinhua News Agency, October 18, 2023.

good social environment for advancing national rejuvenation on all fronts by pursuing Chinese modernization and has also contributed to maintaining global peace and stability.

China's national security has been strengthened across the board. Facing more severe domestic and international challenges, China has applied a holistic approach to national security and steadily improved the leadership, legal, strategy, and policy systems for national security. China's high-quality development has strengthened its material foundations for ensuring high-standard security, which, in turn, has ensured its high-quality development. China has intensified the fight against terrorism and separatism and ensured nonoccurrence of terrorist incidents and violence in the country for six consecutive years[1]. China has also ensured sustained peace and security in Hong Kong and Macao and the successful implementation of the One Country, Two Systems policy. Thanks to comprehensive measures and continued efforts, the whole of society has been mobilized to safeguard national security, and the people's line of defense has been consolidated to ensure security in all areas.

Living standards have been improved in all aspects. The CPC has strengthened social development, with a focus on ensuring and improving the people's wellbeing. It has continued to make every possible effort, year by year, to tackle one issue after another, all to ensure people's access to childcare, education, employment, medical services, elderly care, housing, and social assistance. Since 1949, the average life expectancy in China has risen from below 35 years to 78.2 years, and the illiteracy rate has dropped from as high as 80 percent to 2.67 percent. All of this has ensured that the people are leading fulfilling, happy and secure lives. Since the 18th CPC National Congress, China has created more

---

[1] "The Ministry of Public Security: China maintains a record of zero terrorist incidents and violence for 6 consecutive years," People.cn, January 10, 2023. http://society.people.com.cn/n1/2023/0110/c1008-32603569.html

than 130 million urban jobs and established the world's largest education, social security, and healthcare systems.

China's system and capacity for governance have been steadily modernized. China has accelerated the reform of its social governance system. Since the CPC's 18th National Congress, innovative steps have been taken to strengthen social management, promote innovations in the social governance system, develop a new model of social governance, and build a community of social governance. Guided by the principle of shared responsibilities and shared benefits, more stakeholders have become involved in governance. By the end of 2021, all urban communities in China had ensured access to comprehensive public service facilities, compared to 82 percent of urban communities at the end of the 13th Five-Year Plan period (2016-2020). The figure for rural communities increased from 31.8 percent to 84.6 percent in the same time frame. By the end of the 14th Five-Year Plan period (2021-2025), all urban and rural communities in China are expected to have access to comprehensive public service facilities.

Chapter Two

Practical Approaches to Chinese Modernization

Our experience proves that Chinese modernization works and that it is the only correct path to building a great country and rejuvenating the nation.[①]

—Xi Jinping

The success of Chinese modernization didn't simply fall from the sky, nor did it spring from the ground. Rather, it has been achieved, step by step, by the CPC, dedicated to its founding mission as it has led the Chinese people, one generation after another, in a concerted and solid effort to persevere through tough times.

In leading and advancing Chinese modernization, the CPC has exercised

---

① "Xi Jinping addresses the opening of a study session at the Party school of the CPC Central Committee," Xinhua News Agency, February 7, 2023.

overall leadership, upheld a people-centered development philosophy, followed a path of independence and self-reliance and a policy of reform and opening up, developed new quality productive forces, and emphasized a systematic approach, so as to ensure that Chinese modernization is making steady progress.

1. Leadership by the CPC Is the Fundamental Underpinning of Chinese Modernization

Chinese modernization is socialist modernization under the leadership of the CPC. The CPC's leadership is directly involved in the fundamental direction and the ultimate success or failure of Chinese modernization. It is the fundamental underpinning of Chinese modernization.

1) Ensuring the smooth advancement of Chinese modernization along the right path

The banner shows the way, and which road the way takes us down determines our destiny. What banner to fly and what road to walk are of fundamental importance to a country's development. The CPC holds high the great banner of socialism with Chinese characteristics and unswervingly follows the road of socialism with Chinese characteristics, thus ensuring that Chinese modernization advances smoothly along the right path.

The CPC has steadily advanced theoretical innovation on the basis of practice, thus providing sound theoretical guidance for Chinese modernization. It has endeavored to modernize the system and capacity for governance, thus providing strong institutional guarantees that can support Chinese modernization. It has continued to promote the creative transformation and development of fine traditional Chinese culture and the development of modern Chinese civilization, thus creating a powerful source of inspiration for Chinese modernization.

As Xi Jinping has said, "Chinese modernization will have bright prospects and prosper only if we unswervingly uphold the leadership of the Party. Otherwise, we will veer off course, forget ourselves, or even commit catastrophic errors."[1]

2) Making steady and sustained efforts to secure the goals of Chinese modernization

The CPC has stayed true to its founding mission of pursuing happiness for the people and rejuvenation for the nation, and it has always worked to pursue both its lofty ideals and tangible, incremental progress. Once its goals are set, the CPC will never stop until they are met. This has enabled it to transcend the fate of some countries to suffer endless strife between political parties and fickle policy platforms.

The advancement of Chinese modernization has been a relay race through history. In particular, since the launch of the reform and opening up policy, China has been firm in pursuing the goals of modernization, steadily improving and enriching them through practice. At the 20th CPC National Congress convened in 2022, an inspiring blueprint was drawn up for building China into a great modern socialist country in all respects and advancing national rejuvenation on all fronts through a Chinese path to modernization. This spirit of generation after generation tenaciously fighting to achieve the nation's goals is profound evidence of the CPC's strategic resolve and institutional strengths.

3) Creating a mighty force to advance Chinese modernization

Scattered, we are hopeless; together, we are strong. In a country with such a large population and complex conditions as China, in order to rally all forces to

---

[1] "Xi Jinping addresses the opening of a study session at the Party school of the CPC Central Committee," Xinhua News Agency, February 7, 2023.

pursue modernization, there must be a united political party.

From a small political party with just a few dozen members, the CPC has grown into a party with more than 98 million members, a party that governs a country of more than 1.4 billion people. The CPC has always attached great importance to achieving unity by relying on common ideals and convictions, a tight organizational system, a Party-wide sense of consciousness, and strict discipline and rules. The CPC will continue using its latest achievements in adapting Marxism to the Chinese context and the needs of the times to arm all of its members, so as to achieve unity in thinking, will, and action.

Chinese modernization is the cause of the hundreds of millions of Chinese people, and the people are the agents of Chinese modernization. The CPC has its roots in the people, and the people are its lifeblood and its source of strength. The CPC has no special interests of its own, nor does it represent any interest group, any power bloc, or any privileged class. Rather, it has always represented the fundamental interests of all of the Chinese people. With a stirring vision of Chinese modernization, the CPC has inspired, motivated, and rallied the people and promoted harmony among political parties, ethnic groups, religions, and Chinese both at home and abroad. It has thus brought the sons and daughters of the Chinese nation in and outside China together to strive in unity, creating a mighty force for building a modern socialist country in all respects.

2. Upholding a People-Centered Development Philosophy

Development is the eternal theme of human society. Modernization serves the people's longing for a better life and is a goal pursued by all countries across the world. Rooted in a people-centered development philosophy, Chinese modernization aims to protect the people's interests, advance their well-being, and ensure that development is for the people and by the people and that its fruits are shared equitably by all the people.

1) Upholding development as the CPC's top priority in governance

The goals of modernization can only be achieved through development, and the CPC has "pursued development as its top priority in governance." Keenly aware that "development is of paramount importance" and that "development holds the key to solving all of China's problems," the CPC has "made dedicated efforts to pursue development" as the central task of advancing Chinese modernization.

China is a latecomer in the process of global modernization. Catching up is no easy task, and only a few countries have succeeded. Many countries that started late in pursuing modernization have landed themselves in all sorts of development dilemmas. In the end, how to maintain sustained and healthy economic development is a fundamental challenge facing every country in the world.

Thanks to more than 40 years of rapid development since the launch of reform and opening up, China's economy has grown fast, and it now comfortably ranks as the world's second largest. In 2023, China's per capita GDP reached 89,358 yuan, an increase of 5.4 percent from the previous year. When calculated at the average annual exchange rate, it amounts to roughly US$12,700, maintaining a record above US$12,000 for three consecutive years.[①] China's economic achievements have been widely recognized.

2) Meeting the people's growing needs for a better life

Bringing maximum benefit to the people is what governance is all about. Guided by the people-centered development philosophy, Chinese modernization aims to ensure that development is for the people and by the people and that its

---

[①] "The Underlying Trend of Economic Recovery and Growth in the Long Run Remains Unchanged in China," Leading Party Members Groups of the National Bureau of Statistics, Qiushi Journal, 3rd issue, 2024.

fruits are shared by the people. It is pursued to meet the people's growing needs for a better life and equitably deliver the benefits of modernization to all.

This country is its people, and the people are the country. The Party has fought to establish and defend the People's Republic, and in doing so it has been defending the will of the people. As Xi Jinping said, "Our goal is to see that the people's aspirations for a better life are fulfilled," and, "The Communist Party is here to do things for the people to make life better for them day by day, year by year."

Guided by this philosophy, China has made every effort to support and improve the people's livelihoods through development. It has taken forceful and effective measures to address issues that are important in the life of the people, such as education, employment, healthcare, social security, and social stability. As a result, the people feel more fulfilled, happier, and more secure.

3) Following the overarching guidelines for China's development

Chinese modernization is an ongoing endeavor that will continue for a long time to come. We have seen that Chinese modernization is a broad path to building a great country and rejuvenating the nation. But this broad path may not always be smooth, and our goals cannot be achieved overnight. It will require a lot of hard work to turn the grand blueprint of Chinese modernization into a reality.

How can we continue to make miraculous achievements in development as we forge ahead on our journey ahead? China's answer is to embrace a new stage of development, apply a new philosophy of development, create a new pattern of development, and promote high-quality development. This means embracing a new stage of development to build a modern socialist country in all respects, applying a new philosophy of innovative, coordinated, green, open, and shared development, moving faster to foster a new pattern of development that focuses on the domestic economy but features positive interplay between domestic and international economic flows, and continue promoting high-quality development.

The new stage of development tells us where we are now, the new philosophy of development lays down the principles that guide our way forward, and the new pattern of development shows us the path to follow. The three are unified under the theme of high-quality development. High-quality development is our top priority in building a modern socialist country in all respects. In the past, China pursued development to meet the basic needs of its people. In the future, China's development will focus more on ensuring the well-being of its people. China will constantly improve the quality and effectiveness of its development.

3. Independence and Self-Reliance Are the Only Way

Chinese modernization is a distinctive path that the CPC has blazed in leading the Chinese people to independently carry out long-term explorations and unremitting struggles. It is a path that suits China's conditions and meets the needs of the Chinese people. This path is determined by China's national conditions and nature as a socialist country as well as the times, historical context, and external environment in which Chinese modernization is pursued.

1) Making concerted efforts to modernize China under the strong leadership of the CPC

As a developing country with a population of more than 1.4 billion, China naturally faces many complex issues and problems as it pursues prosperity for all in the process of modernization. These issues and problems can be resolved only through the strong leadership of the CPC and the concerted efforts of the Chinese people. Only by leveraging the political strengths of socialism can we motivate the people and pool resources to launch major initiatives, thus creating powerful synergies for achieving modernization.

2) Forging our own path through the arduous explorations of the Chinese people

Some developing countries once hoped to copy the Western path to modernization, but they all ended in failure due to ignorance of their own national conditions. In the 1980s and onwards, some Latin American countries accepted the policy recommendations of the Washington Consensus and introduced neoliberal reforms to varying degrees. Although some gains were made in their economic transitions, many major problems emerged, such as the loss of government control over the economy and growing social polarization.

Unlike these countries, China has followed its own path to modernization. By staying connected to its concrete reality and through arduous exploration, China has set clear goals, tasks, and essential requirements for Chinese modernization. This path to modernization is rooted in China's reality and has distinctive Chinese features.

3) Only by maintaining independence and self-reliance can China be free from others' control

To grow strong, we must first and foremost maintain independence and self-reliance. Leaving the future and destiny of one's country in the hands of others can only derail its pursuit of modernization. Even worse, it could lead to a country's subjugation by others or even its disintegration. For more than 100 years, the CPC has rallied the Chinese people and led them in unyielding struggles, overcoming many unimaginable difficulties and winning one great victory after another. As China's economy has continued to grow, the living standards of more than 1.4 billion people have been steadily raised, and moderate prosperity has been achieved in all respects. All of this has further consolidated the CPC's place as the governing party, and the giant ship of socialism with Chinese characteristics has continued to sail forward. It is independence and self-reliance that have made all these achievements possible.

4. Reform and Opening Up Is a Crucial Move

A review of the history of global modernization shows that economic modernization is core to a country's modernization and serves as its material foundation. It is also an important source of power driving modernization as a whole. China's reform and opening up process, which began in 1978, was a crucial move that has enabled China to take great strides to catch up with the times and has made China what it is today. Reform and opening up is therefore of vital importance to continuing to advance Chinese modernization.

1) Without reform and opening up, China would not be what it is today

Before reform and opening up started, China had become stagnant and lagged behind the times. With tremendous political courage, Deng Xiaoping, the chief architect of China's socialist reform, opening up, and modernization, called for the launch of the reform and opening up policy. He said, "If we don't reform now, our modernization program and socialist cause will be doomed." Deng Xiaoping regarded reform and opening up as an important way to unleash and develop China's productive forces and as an initiative that was crucial to the future and destiny of socialism in China. Since the launch of reform and opening up, the CPC has led the Chinese people in freeing their minds, seeking truth from facts, and boldly carrying out experiments and reforms. By making timely adjustments to the relations of production that were not compatible with the development of the productive forces, China caught up with the times in great strides and opened up a vast new horizon.

Wuyi Village is in Chengxi Sub-district, Yiwu, Zhejiang Province. When a visitor sees Wuyi's rows of beautifully designed new Chinese-style townhouses with white walls and black tiles, one may think that they have entered a neighborhood of urban villas. Yiwu was among the first places in China to pilot the reform of separating the ownership, qualification, and use rights of rural residential plots. While ensuring that every household had a house, the reform went further to allow the transfer of residential plot qualification rights and interests between people from different villages. Since this pilot was launched, reforms have given rural residents more property rights and put 10 billion yuan of dormant rural assets to work, giving new impetus to rural development.

At a time when the global economic recovery is sluggish, only countries with good business environments will attract investment, enjoy thriving business, and demonstrate strong economic resilience and self-sustaining momentum. China has promoted reforms to streamline administration, delegate powers, and improve regulation and services. This has created a market environment of fair competition in which state-owned enterprises grow vigorously, private businesses blaze new trails, and foreign companies do not hesitate to invest. During the COVID-19 pandemic, local governments in China rolled out a full range of policies to help market entities survive and grow.

China's ranking in the World Bank's Doing Business Report jumped nearly 50 places from 78th in 2018 to 31st in 2020. This put it among the top 10 economies that had made the greatest improvements in their business environments for the second year in a row.

Reform and opening up is an ongoing endeavor that will continue for a long time to come. Reaching a new crossroads in history, China finds itself facing broad and profound changes in both its internal and external environments. Reform has entered uncharted waters and will inevitably encounter tough challenges. Going forward, China must deepen reform and opening up on all fronts in order to realize Chinese modernization. Of particular importance is the continuation of reforms to grow the socialist market economy, to give full play to its institutional strengths, and to promote both an efficient market and a well-functioning government.

2) China adheres to the right direction, stance, and principles in carrying out reform

China is now deepening reform across the board, but this does not mean that everything will change. China adheres to the right direction, stance, and principles in carrying out reform. It will firmly change what should and can be changed, and it will firmly resist changing what should not and cannot be changed.

Socialism is the fundamental direction of China's reform, and the people's position is the most fundamental stance of reform. The most salient principle guiding China's reform is the leadership of the CPC. This leadership is the defining feature of socialism with Chinese characteristics, and it is the greatest strength of the system of socialism with Chinese characteristics. This direction, stance, and principle must be adhered to and should never be changed.

While upholding and developing the socialist system, China carries out reform to change the parts and elements of the relations of production that are out of step with China's productive forces and the parts of the superstructure that are incompatible with the economic foundation. This reform is pursued to strike a balance between the "visible hand" and the "invisible hand," so as to ensure the steady improvement of socialism with Chinese characteristics and the growth of China's productive forces.

China has developed new ways to regulate market activities, and it has fully implemented fair competition policies against monopoly and unfair competition. For example, in the face of global challenges such as the regulation of monopoly capital, while fully leveraging the positive role of capital as a factor of production, China has improved its legal system and strengthened law-based regulation. It has created a "traffic light" to prevent capital from being diverted away from the real economy and blindly expanding. All of these changes will further enable capital to play an important role in promoting the development of productive forces, creating social wealth, and ensuring and improving the people's well-being.

3) China will pursue high-standard opening up to promote reform and development

Opening up to the outside world has boosted China's economic and social development. It has played a key role in promoting reform and development, thus enabling China to make continuous advances in development.

China began its process of reform and opening up in 1978, opening its doors to the world. Following the trend of global development, China seized the strategic opportunities created by economic globalization and acceded to the World Trade Organization. By relying on its own efforts and riding the tide of global development, China has achieved economic take-off.

Since the beginning of the new era in 2012, China has further opened itself, more actively pursued the opening up strategy, and built a globally oriented network of high-standard free trade areas, thus promoting opening up on a larger scale, in more areas, and at a higher level.

Craig Allen, president of the United States-China Business Council, remarked that despite challenges, cooperation between US companies and their Chinese counterparts is extremely resilient. According to Allen, the total volume of trade in goods between the US and China reached a record high in 2022, and US exports to China supported nearly one million jobs in the US.[1] A survey by the European Union (EU) Chamber of Commerce in China shows that more than 60 percent of EU companies surveyed consider China one of their top three investment destinations. Jörg Wuttke, president of the EU Chamber of Commerce in China, said that the choice of EU companies to invest in China fully reflects their confidence in China's open market and that they hope to be a part of China's development story.

Going forward, China will open even wider to the rest of the world.

China will continue to improve its legal system for intellectual property protection and formulate and improve laws and regulations on IP protection in the age of the digital economy. The Foreign Investment Law and its implementation regulations have been adopted, a management system based on

---

[1] "Growth drivers, Confidence, Opportunities: insights from global financial and economic leaders on China's economic growth prospects," Xinhua News Agency, March 26, 2023.

pre-establishment national treatment and a negative list has been implemented, and the negative list for foreign investment has been repeatedly shortened.

China will continue to pursue high-standard opening up and expand the level of opening up based on goods and factor flows to institutional opening up in terms of rules, regulations, management, and standards. It will remain committed to economic globalization, promote trade and investment liberalization and facilitation, boost the momentum and vitality of its modernization through opening up, and continue to create new opportunities for the world through its development.

5. Accelerating the Development of New Quality Productive Forces

To build a modern socialist country in all respects, China must, first and foremost, pursue high-quality development. Cultivating new quality productive forces stands as an intrinsic requirement and an important focus of this endeavor. Primarily driven by innovation, new quality productive forces break free from traditional economic growth modes and productivity development paths, feature high technology, efficiency and quality, and represent an advanced form of productivity aligned with the new development philosophy. They are shaped by revolutionary technological breakthroughs, innovative allocation of production factors, and profound industrial transformation and upgrading. Improvements to labor forces, means of labor, subjects of labor and their optimal combination constitute the fundamental elements, and a significant increase in total factor productivity is the core hallmark. With innovation as the trait and quality as the key, new quality productive forces are advanced productivity in essence.[①] Accelerating the development of new quality productive forces is a strategic

---

[①] "Xi Jinping stresses development of new quality productive forces, high-quality development," Xinhua News Agency, February 1, 2024.

decision made to seize the commanding heights in a new round of global scientific and technological revolution and industrial transformation, open up new areas and new arenas in development, cultivate fresh growth drivers, and build up nascent competitive advantages.

1) Scientific and technological innovation is essential

Scientific and technological innovation can generate new industries, novel business models and fresh growth drivers, and is essential for the development of new quality productive forces. It is thus imperative to boost scientific and technological innovation, particularly original and disruptive innovations, speed up efforts to attain greater self-reliance and strength in science and technology, boost emerging strategic industries, and rigorously grow future industries.

According to the Global Innovation Index 2023, a report released by the World Intellectual Property Organization (WIPO), China holds the 12th position and is the sole middle-income economy among the top 30 economies. China also secures three seats in the world's five biggest science and technology cluster ranking. In 2023, the country's total research and development expenditure reached 3.3 trillion yuan, or 2.64 percent of its GDP[①]. The principal role of enterprises in innovation was further reinforced. China boasts approximately 400,000 high-tech enterprises, eight times of 2012's figure of 49,000. It now leads the world in terms of the number of top 100 global scientific and technological innovation clusters.

At the National SuperComputer Center in Tianjin Binhai New Area, a powerful supercomputer is working around the clock. This is China's first petaflop supercomputer, which runs as fast as hundreds of thousands of connected laptops running together.

[①] The Statistical Communiqué of the People's Republic of China on the 2023 National Economic and Social Development, the National Bureau of Statistics, February 29, 2024.

From the release of the first global map of Mars to the development of an exaflop supercomputer, China has continued to step up original and pioneering scientific and technological research, breaking new ground in innovation. In recent years, it has strengthened basic research and original innovation to remove technological bottlenecks, making breakthroughs in some core technologies in key areas.

China has made continuous efforts to scale new heights in science and technology, with achievements such as the launch of the Shenzhou spacecraft, the commissioning of the Jiaolong deep-sea manned submersible, the success of the Chang'e lunar probe series, the landing of the Tianwen-1 probe on Mars, the deployment of the BeiDou Navigation Satellite System, and the launch of the Mozi quantum science satellite.

The modernization of science and technology is key to Chinese modernization. By accelerating the development of new quality productive forces, China lays solid material and technological foundations for its modernization and pursuit of high-quality development.

2) Talent is the primary resource

Talent is the most active and decisive factor in developing new quality productive forces. In order to meet the requirements for developing new quality productive forces, China is promoting the forming of a virtuous cycle among education, science and technology, and personnel training, enhancing the working mechanisms, intensifying efforts in nurturing talent, and improving incentives in income distribution. These efforts aim to improve the conditions for nurturing talent, create a favorable atmosphere that champions innovation and allows for failure, and turn the "key variables" of innovators into the "greatest increments" for accelerating the development of new quality productive forces.

In Qingdao, a coast city in east China's Shandong Province, a LiDAR can turn wind field information within a range of 10,000 meters into visualized data through three-dimensional scanning, which can not only observe wind but also predict it. This technology was developed over 20 years ago at the Qingdao-based Ocean University of China, and had provided meteorological support during the Beijing Winter Olympics and scientific expeditions to Mount Everest. However, this technology was not applied outside the laboratory in a timely manner. In recent years, Shandong has optimized the allocation of resource elements, supporting enterprises in collaborating with universities and research institutes to achieve breakthroughs in technologies, providing research personnel with marketing teams, promoting the integration of experimental technological products with application scenarios, introducing angel investments, analyzing and judging research results according to market logic, and promoting the market application of research results. Today, the wind LiDAR has empowered a number of industries. In just five years, the annual output of Qingdao Leice Transient Technology Co., Ltd., which focuses on the research and development, manufacturing, and related technical services of the entire LiDAR system and key LiDAR components, has exceeded 100 million yuan, with an average annual growth rate of 70 percent[1].

China's full-time equivalent of research and development personnel had increased from 3.247 million person-years in 2012 to 6.354 million person-years in 2022, ranking first in the world. The international academic influence of the country's top scientific and technological talent continues to increase, with the number of the world's highly cited scientists increasing from 111 person-times in 2014 to 1,169 person-times in 2022, ranking second in the world[2].

---

[1] "A report on Shandong's efforts in accelerating the development of new quality productive forces," Xinhua News Agency, January 28, 2024.

[2] "China's full-time equivalent of research and development personnel increases to 6.354 million," Xinhua News Agency, December 15, 2023.

3) Developing new quality productive forces based on local conditions

China is a large country with a big population, with resource endowments and development levels varying significantly in different parts of the country. The development of new quality productive forces in China does not mean neglecting or abandoning traditional industries. Instead, it means development based on local conditions, selectively promoting the development of new industries, new business models, and new growth drivers, using new technologies to transform and upgrade traditional industries, and making industries higher-end, smarter, and more eco-friendly.

Mechanical arms move in an orderly manner in the air, cutting edges, conducting quality inspection, labeling... In the rare earth steel cold-rolled sheet factory of Baogang Group, nobody is working there. However, all the equipment is working, revealing an automated, smart, and informationized factory. Facing the significant downward pressure on the steel industry in recent years, the Group, with the support of local policies and its own comprehensive transformation, has not only turned losses into profits but also found a new opportunity for transformation by leveraging the rapid development of new energy.

To accelerate the development of new quality productive forces, southwestern China's Guizhou Province is actively promoting the opening of various industries' application scenarios to Huawei Cloud. Currently, it has selected eight major industries of liquor, coal mining, chemical industry, non-ferrous metals, electricity, new materials, steel, building materials, as well as four areas of urban smart upgrading, rural digitalization, tourism scenario innovation, and government convenience services. The province is deepening the application of Huawei Cloud Pangu large models in key industry scenarios.

6. Advancing Chinese Modernization as a Systematic Endeavor

Chinese modernization is an all-embracing modernization that covers all areas, including the economy, politics, culture, society, and ecological conservation. This endeavor is a multi-dimensional one, involving reform, development, and stability, the governance of the Party, the country, and the military, domestic and foreign affairs, and national defense. It is a process of transformation that will lead to the advancement of society as a whole. Accordingly, the pursuit of Chinese modernization calls for making efforts across many sectors, links, and levels. We must take into account all factors, plan systematically, and advance Chinese modernization as a whole.

1) Making systematic plans to advance Chinese modernization

Advancing Chinese modernization means achieving a broad and profound social transformation. In this endeavor, a single move may affect everything. Therefore, it is necessary to make systematic plans at the macro level.

In the report to the 20th CPC National Congress, a top-level and strategic decision was made to pursue Chinese modernization as the Party's central task on the new journey in this new era. Strategic plans were made for building China into a great modern socialist country in all respects, and clear goals for each stage, as well as a timetable and roadmap for achieving these goals, were set. The report also laid out systematic and well-considered plans to advance work in 12 areas, including speeding up the creation of a new development pattern, implementing the strategy for invigorating China through science and education, advancing whole-process people's democracy, exercising law-based governance on all fronts, and modernizing China's national security system and capacity.

Advancing Chinese modernization is a pioneering cause that has never been attempted before. Many of our tasks have no precedent to follow, many unknown areas need to be explored, and many undertakings require progress through exploration, growth through practice, and advancement through innovation. In advancing this cause, the CPC has paid particular attention to both top-level design and practical exploration. It works to see that top-level design plays the leading, planning, and guidance roles. At the same time, the CPC has been constantly freeing its mind and making bold explorations, "crossing the river by feeling for the stone." It supports and encourages trials and pilot programs on the ground, such as making Shanghai Pudong New Area a pacesetter of socialist modernization, building a demonstration zone for realizing common prosperity through high-quality development in Zhejiang Province, and establishing national pilot zones in Fujian, Jiangxi, Guizhou, and Hainan provinces for ecological conservation. Both top-level design and practical exploration have ensured sustained and steady progress in advancing Chinese modernization.

2) Taking into account all factors to advance Chinese modernization

Advancing Chinese modernization is a complex and challenging task, and it requires a systematic and holistic approach. Therefore, it has been important to take into account all factors and properly handle the following major relationships.

Enhancing efficiency while promoting fairness. In pursuing modernization, China has continued to boost its economic strength and unleash social dynamism, thus achieving a higher degree of efficiency than the capitalist system and creating miraculous economic growth. At the same time, it has upheld social fairness, applied a people-centered development philosophy, paid special attention to promoting prosperity for all, and achieved coordinated regional and urban-rural development to ensure that everyone has the opportunity to participate in the modernization process and enjoy its benefits.

Advancing reform and development while ensuring stability. In pursuing modernization, China has energized its development and deepened reform on all fronts to address issues of interests that concern the people most. It has endeavored to develop whole-process people's democracy, built extensive consensus in society, developed new approaches to improve social governance at the community level, and fully motivated its people and released their creativity. At the same time, China has maintained social order and stability. In determining the intensity of reform and the pace of development, it has taken into account the level of public acceptance of change, and it has maintained both the energized development and order and stability, thereby creating a miracle of sustained social stability.

Promoting development while ensuring security. China has always proactively pursued modernization. It has seized major historical and strategic opportunities to accede into the WTO, integrate itself into economic globalization, and actively unleash a new wave of scientific and technological revolutions and industrial transformations. At the same time, it has continued to guard against and mitigate major risks, improve its national security system, and ensure the security of major industrial and supply chains. China has remained on guard against various "black swan" and "gray rhino" events that could occur at any time.

3) Advancing Chinese modernization as a whole

Chinese modernization is an all-embracing modernization that encompasses the economic, political, cultural, social, and ecological spheres. These five spheres are not unrelated; rather, they form an organic whole in which they complement each other and are highly connected. We should not expect that a breakthrough in any one sphere will bring us modernization. Only by advancing them all together can we move forward.

Modernization within each of the individual spheres also needs to be advanced in a holistic way. Why has China, in its pursuit of modernization, completed in several decades the process of industrialization that took developed countries more than 200 years to complete? The reason is that it has taken a development path different from that taken by the developed countries of the West. Western countries have pursued development in the order of industrialization, urbanization, agricultural modernization, and then informatization, one at a time. China, on the other hand, has pursued industrialization, informatization, urbanization, and agricultural modernization all at the same time.

Of course, we need to look farther and adopt a broad perspective as we make advances on multiple fronts. This approach does not seek uniformity in advancement, but rather gradual, step-by-step progress on the basis of various conditions. It seeks both overall progress and breakthroughs in key areas, with overall progress as the ultimate goal. Advancing Chinese modernization is a historical process that requires the unremitting efforts of one generation after another.

Take, for instance, China's reform and opening up. China's reform began in rural areas before moving to cities, and it was first carried out in the economic sector and then extended to other fields. China's opening up began in the south, particularly in the southeastern coastal areas, and it gradually expanded to cover the north, and the central and western inland regions. This opening up was gradually expanded in terms of direction, level, and area. Over 40 years later, China's reform and opening up has continued to unfold in both breadth and depth. This represents the overall progress of Chinese modernization.

Advancing Chinese modernization is an arduous, complex, and challenging endeavor, and various difficulties, both foreseeable and unforeseeable, are bound to arise. Keenly aware of this, the CPC has always taken a systematic approach, with the understanding that all things are interconnected, part of a complete system, and constantly evolving. Taking this approach, it endeavors to properly manage the relationships between the whole and the parts, the immediate and the long-term, the macro and the micro, the primary and the secondary, and the particular and the general. The CPC has also steadily improved its ability to think dialectically, to deal with worst-case scenarios, and to conduct governance and leadership. All of this has provided continued impetus for advancing Chinese modernization in a systematic way.

Chapter Three

Defining Features of Chinese Modernization

For any country to achieve modernization, it needs not only to follow the general laws governing the process, but more importantly consider its own national conditions and unique features. Chinese modernization contains elements that are common to the modernization processes of all countries, but it is more characterized by features that are unique to the Chinese context.[①]

–Xi Jinping

Modernization is a comprehensive concept that is compatible with the mode of industrialized production and includes marketization, democratization, legalization, urbanization and other elements. Since the industrial revolution, in

---

[①] "Xi Jinping addresses the opening of a study session at the Party school of the CPC Central Committee," Xinhua News Agency, February 7, 2023.

the pursuit of modernization, all countries have common characteristics in the transition from tradition to modernity. In the meantime, they also have their own distinctive features.

It has been shown that the path to modernization a country chooses is determined by many factors, such as its historical traditions, social system, development conditions, and external environment. Taking its national conditions into consideration, China has pioneered a new path toward modernization with its characteristics and made successive remarkable achievements that have attracted world attention, displaying unique features of Chinese modernization to the world.

1. Modernization of a Large Population

An enormous population and large development disparities between urban and rural areas and among different regions have long been a reality for China. China is working to achieve modernization for more than 1.4 billion people, a number larger than the combined population of all developed countries in the world today. Chinese modernization will be unprecedented in history in terms of its scale, the number of people that benefit from it, and the formidable challenges along the way.

1) The greatest modernization benefiting the largest population

China, a large developing country, has a population that outnumbers the combined populations of all developed countries. Therefore, Chinese modernization is the modernization of huge population. In comparison, Britain had a population of less than six million at the outset of the First Industrial Revolution. The American population was close to 80 million during the Second Industrial Revolution. By 2019, the total population of countries and regions that have achieved modernization worldwide has not exceeded one billion. With such a large population, as China develops into a modern country, the world's landscape of modernization will be completely changed. Hence, Xi Jinping pointed out that Chinese modernization is the most difficult and the greatest.[1]

Since the CPC's 18th National Congress, the Party has undertaken the most extensive and aggressive anti-poverty campaign in the history of humanity. With this, the CPC has turned China into a prosperous society in all respects, benefiting the largest population in the history of human development. Chinese modernization not only expands the avenue toward modernization for developing countries, but also offers Chinese insight and solutions to problems facing humanity. Martin Jacques, a British scholar and a visiting researcher at the Institute of International Relations of Tsinghua University noted that, "Its (China's) demographic size, its sense of independence and identity, its rich historical inheritance, and a remarkable political leadership enable it to achieve Chinese path to modernization." He said, "We now find ourselves at a great historical juncture. Now modernization is no longer for a tiny sliver of humanity but is increasingly accessible to the great majority... While the Age of the West was the Age of the Small Minority, the Age of China will be the Age of the Great Majority."[2]

2) Abundant human resources and super-large market scale creating development potential

Since the policy of reform and opening up was introduced in 1978, plenty of rural surplus labor was transferred from the agricultural sector to non-agricultural sectors, in particular to manufacturing, yielding remarkable "demographic dividends," and promoting the relocation of resources between

---

[1] "Strive in unity to build a modern socialist country in all respects: on the successful conclusion of the 20th CPC National Congress," Xinhua News Agency, October 23, 2022.
[2] "Chinese modernization leads to Age of Great Majority: Martin Jacques," Global Times, May 12, 2023, https://opinion.huanqiu.com/article/4CrBgxTvuxF.

rural and urban areas, as well as among different regions and industries. Over the past decade, while speeding up the transformation and upgrading of the manufacturing sector, China has energetically developed new forms of business, such as the cyber economy and platform economy, and witnessed a significant influx of young workers into tertiary industries. By the end of 2022, China had a labor force of nearly 900 million. In recent years, an average of over 12 million urban jobs has been created annually.[①] Since the 18th CPC National Congress, China has adopted an employment-first policy and eliminated unjustified restrictions and discrimination that undermine equal employment, ensuring everyone has the opportunity to pursue a career through hard work. The average per capita disposable income in China increased from 18,311 yuan in 2013 to 39,218 yuan in 2023, driving an upswing in consumption. A large body of consumers, coupled with their strong purchasing power, continue to promote the transformation and upgrading of consumption patterns, giving shape to an enormous, unified market and propelling the remarkable development of infrastructure, transportation, and the information and service industries. In the pursuit of Chinese modernization, the abundance of human resources and the vast market serve as invaluable assets, fueling powerful momentum for high-quality development.

Meituan, a Chinese network technology retail company, has provided a model for solving China's employment challenges arising from its large population. This company now provides a wide range of over 200 types of consumer services, including take-out, catering, hotel accommodation, and travel, serving over 9.3 million businesses and 680 million customers at home while attracting a significant number of employees. This enterprise boasts an astonishing fleet of delivery workers, In 2022, over 6.24 million delivery workers

---

[①] "With over 12 mln urban jobs to be created, how to stabilize the employment market in 2024?", Xinhua News Agent, March 5, 2024.

earned income through Meituan's platforms, and the daily count of active delivery workers surpassed 1 million. From 2018 to 2023, the number of delivery workers registered on the platform and come from key counties receiving government assistance for rural revitalization increased from 120,000 to 395,000, covering all 160 such counties in China. China boasts a mass of Internet companies and renowned e-commerce platforms, such as Taobao, JD.com, Pinduoduo, Dianping, and Ctrip, in addition to Meituan. They not only make up a gigantic online market but also take in a substantial workforce.

3) An urbanization process of the largest scale and fastest pace in world history

Cities play important roles in modernization. Prior to the introduction of the reform and opening up policy, the urban population in China made up less than 18 percent. Since then, China has initiated an urbanization process of the largest scale and fastest pace in world history. Now, in many regions in east China, such as Shanghai, Guangdong, Jiangsu, and Zhejiang, the urban and rural areas have been integrated. Thanks to the persistent implementation of large-scale development policy and the stimulation effects of major cities such as Chongqing, Chengdu, and Xi'an, the western region has witnessed thriving city clusters, accelerated urban-rural integration, and a narrowing urban-rural gap. Statistics show that the share of permanent urban residents in the total population reached 66.16 percent in 2023.[①] In accordance with the 14th Five-Year Plan for Economic and Social Development (2021–2025) promulgated in 2022, China will adhere to the path of new urbanization with Chinese characteristics, advance people-centered new urbanization, and leverage the role of city clusters and metropolitan areas to promote the coordinated development of cities of different sizes and

---

① The Statistical Communiqué of the People's Republic of China on the 2023 National Economic and Social Development, the National Bureau of Statistics, February 29, 2024.

small towns with their own distinctive features, thus enabling more people to enjoy higher-quality urban life.

With upgraded rural infrastructure and the implementation of urban-rural integration policies, many rural areas in China are no longer associated with outdated productivity. Instead, they have become new stages for urban talent to pursue entrepreneurship and carry out innovation activities, and the land of happiness that they admire. The human resources, capital, technology from cities combined with the strength of land and labor in rural areas inject fresh elements and vitality into the traditional agricultural sector during its transformation. This synergy not only meets the evolving demands of cities and urban residents, but also paves the way for the creation of innovative agricultural industries.

4) Addressing diverse and intricate needs of a vast population

When a minor problem is magnified within the context of China's massive population of over 1.4 billion people, it undoubtedly escalates into a major challenge. With China's large population comes diverse interest demands of different regions, sectors, and social groups. The large population also gave rise to immense essential requirement of ensuring the people's wellbeing, including basic needs such as food, healthcare, education, elderly care, and law and order. These pose significant challenges to the advancement of Chinese modernization. In improving people's living standards, China gives top priority to solving the pressing difficulties and problems that concern people the most. China has remained patient in advancing the course of history, taken steady and incremental steps to sustain progress, and turned the challenge posed by a large population into an advantage in scale for the modernization drive.

As a populous country with limited farmland, China always places food security above all. In recent years, it has taken strict and standardized measures to offset cultivated land used for other purposes and made steady and orderly efforts to maintain the total area of arable land, in order to ensure the area of farmland remains above the red line of 1.8 billion mu (120 million hectares), giving the Chinese people a secure food supply. Up until now, China has developed 1 billion mu of high-standard cropland. We have achieved grain harvests for 20 years on end and seen grain output stay above 650 million tonnes for nine consecutive years. China boasts a self-sufficiency rate of above 100 percent for staple food. Moreover, the country boasts an average annual per capita grain supply of 490 kilograms, surpassing the globally recognized safety threshold of 400 kilograms.[①]

In terms of ensuring personal safety, China has been regarded as one of the safest countries in the world. The Chinese government has consistently emphasized the comprehensive maintenance of law and order, implementing robust measures to combat organized crime. As a result, there has been a continuous yearly decline in the number of major criminal cases, public security cases, and total criminal cases. As evening falls, urban residents can joyfully engage in leisurely strolls, exercise, and recreational activities in the streets, alleys and parks. On China's video-sharing platform Bilibili, a young foreigner said, "People often overlook the good parts of China, because they neither show tolerance to China nor would like to go there themselves. Safety is one of the good parts of the country."

2. Modernization for the Common Prosperity of All

Achieving common prosperity is a defining feature of socialism with Chinese characteristics and an abiding goal of the Chinese Communists. Chinese modernization aims to ensure that the gains of modernization benefit all people fairly, and constantly satisfy the people's ever-growing needs for a better life. By promoting common prosperity and preventing polarization, China's goal is

---

[①] The Statistical Communiqué of the People's Republic of China on the 2023 National Economic and Social Development, the National Bureau of Statistics, February 29, 2024.

to foster a harmonious and stable society while maintaining steady economic development.

1) "On the road to common prosperity, no one will be left behind"

Looking back on the history of Chinese civilization spanning over 5,000 years, one can observe that the ideal of pursuing common prosperity has been deeply ingrained in China's fine traditional culture. Laozi stated, "Diminish where there is superabundance and supplement where there is deficiency." Confucius said, "Fear not scarcity but inequality." Guan Zhong mentioned that, "The key to running a country is to first enrich its people." A society of "universal harmony" was an ideal illustrated in *The Book of Rites*.

Carrying forward China's fine traditional culture, the CPC makes achieving common prosperity for all one of its major goals. The Party remains committed to the mission that development is for the people and by the people, and that its fruits are shared by the people. Mao Zedong said, "Our prosperity is common prosperity, and our strength is shared by all. Everyone has a part to play in this." Deng Xiaoping emphasized, "Some people and some regions should be allowed to prosper before others, always with the goal of common prosperity." Xi Jinping stated, "The common prosperity that we pursue, both material and cultural, is for all of our people; It is not for a small minority, nor does it imply an absolute equality in income distribution that takes no account of contribution." As a party that emerges from and represents the people, the CPC has dedicated itself to serving the people. Thus, the pursuit of common prosperity for all stands as its long-term aspiration and committed action.

China has finally resolved the problem of absolute poverty, achieved moderate prosperity in all respects, and consistently elevated the quality of life for its people through its ongoing pursuit of modernization. Presently, with a middle-income group exceeding 400 million people and per capita disposable income surpassing 39,000 yuan, China has achieved a historic leap from a low-income country to an upper-middle-income country.

By conducting a trial and presenting a set of data, China vividly exemplifies its approach to achieving common prosperity. As Zhejiang Province strives to become a model of common prosperity through high-quality development, the per capita disposable income of local residents reached 63,800 yuan[①] in 2023, while the ratio of urban income to rural income lowered from 2.37:1 in 2012 to 1.86:1 in 2023.

2) Weaving the world's largest social security net

People's wellbeing is an important indicator and basic component of common prosperity. To achieve modernization, China does everything within its capacity to direct more support, in terms of employment, education, social security, and medical care, toward rural areas, local communities, and underdeveloped regions, as well as helping people living in difficulty, making sure social security programs can meet the people's basic needs.

China now has established the world's largest networks for education, social security, and healthcare. According to statistics, in 2023, the retention rate of nine-year compulsory education and the gross enrollment ratio for senior secondary education reached 95.7% and 91.8% respectively. Basic old-age insurance covered nearly 1.1 billion people, more than 1.3 billion people were enrolled in the basic medical insurance scheme, and 44 million were included in the subsistence allowance and extreme poverty relief scope. There were 1.07 million healthcare institutions across the country in 2023, offering 9.56 billion[②] diagnosis and treatment services per year.

In recent years, in an effort to reduce regional disparities, the central

---

① The Statistical Communiqué on people's livelihood of Zhejiang Province in 2023, Zhejiang Provincial Bureau of Statistics, March 4, 2024.
② The Statistical Communiqué of the People's Republic of China on the 2023 National Economic and Social Development, the National Bureau of Statistics, February 29, 2024.

government of China has consistently increased transfer payments to local governments, prioritizing underdeveloped areas and areas in need, particularly to cover expenditures on education, medical care, and other sectors, which aim to ensure inclusive public services, meet people's essential needs, and guarantee basic living standards for those facing difficulties. In 2023, the transfer payments from the central government to local governments reached 10.29 trillion yuan, marking the highest amount spent in recent years[1].

3) Making the "cake" bigger and sharing it fairly

In the pursuit of Chinese modernization, achieving common prosperity is not an empty political slogan. Rather, it represents a great social reform effort that engages all people striving together under the leadership of the Party. Through the synergy between an efficient market and a well-functioning government, the Chinese people work together to make a bigger "cake" and share it fairly through well-designed institutional arrangements.

The system of income distribution is the foundational system for promoting common prosperity. China emphasizes both efficiency and fairness by establishing an institutional framework under which primary, secondary, and tertiary distribution is well coordinated and mutually complementary. By giving more weight to work remuneration in primary distribution, China has seen personal income essentially growing in step with economic growth, as well as pay rises growing in tandem with increases in productivity. Local governments continue to raise minimum wages in light of local conditions so as to increase the remuneration of workers, in particular those working at the primary level. China improves the policy system for distribution based on factors of production, explores multiple avenues to increase rural incomes, and guarantees the full

---

[1] Report on the Implementation of China's Fiscal Policy in 2023, Ministry of Finance, March 7, 2024.

payment of wages for rural migrant workers. China continues to improve the secondary distribution mechanism, making policy adjustments more intensive and targeted. The individual income tax threshold has been raised from 800 yuan at the outset of the reform and opening up initiative to 5,000 yuan now, and certain expenses, such as children's education, treatment for serious diseases, mortgage interest, and rent, have been included as special deductions for individual income tax, allowing everyone to save more. China also attaches importance to the role of tertiary distribution, by promoting charity programs and encouraging businessmen to actively participate in or launch public welfare and charitable initiatives, so as to ensure the well-to-do shoulder due responsibilities, and show integrity and compassion.

As a long-range objective, the pursuit of common prosperity will be incorporated into the overall process of China's modernization drive and cannot be accomplished overnight. It is China's belief that as long as we continue to promote high-quality development, earnestly address imbalances and inadequacies in development, constantly narrow gaps between urban and rural areas and among regions, and enable everyone to share in the fruits of development, common prosperity for all can be achieved.

3. Modernization of Material and Cultural-ethical Advancement

Chinese modernization aims at both material abundance and cultural-ethical enrichment, allowing both of them to coordinate with and stimulate each other. No country or nation can stand firm in the world if it fails to guide its people with advanced culture, enrich their intellectual lives, and build up its cultural strength.

1) Flourishing cultural programs and industries

In advancing Chinese modernization, great importance is attached to improving the modern public cultural services system, launching new public-benefit cultural programs, expanding the coverage of public cultural services and making them more adaptable to people's needs, and protecting the people's basic cultural rights and interests. China has continually enriched people's cultural lives through the promotion of excellent films, TV programs, dramas, radio plays, and books. Across the country, public museums, libraries, galleries, and cultural centers are opened to the public free of charge, and a national strategy has been formed to foster a love for reading among the people. China has a total of more than 3,300 public libraries[①], more than 100,000 brick-and-mortar bookstores, and 587,000 rural libraries. These have helped facilitate people's love for reading and foster a culture of civility in China.

2) Enhancing civility throughout society

Core values are a bond linking a nation and common moral foundation of a country. Chinese modernization aims to promote core socialist values of prosperity, democracy, civility, harmony, freedom, equality, justice, the rule of law, patriotism, dedication, integrity, and kindness, values which will solidify an intellectual foundation for all Chinese people to strive in unity, foster a pioneering spirit, and cultivate healthy and positive values.

China has worked to foster virtue by example. The country has established a sound system of Party and state awards and honors to promote individuals who exemplify core socialist values for others to follow. In recent years, a number of people were awarded honorary titles of role models of the time, national moral paragons, integrity stars, and outstanding youths in the new era in China. The noble character of these excellent individuals has illuminated society and will inspire generations of Chinese people to strive for excellence and cultivate fine virtues. Inspired by these shining examples, acts of kindness, like rising to the

---

① The Statistical Communiqué of the People's Republic of China on the 2023 National Economic and Social Development, the National Bureau of Statistics, February 29, 2024.

occasion during emergencies, returning lost money, showing respect to the elderly and affection to the young, and lending a helping hand to those in need, have become increasingly common and frequent in Chinese society. All these contribute to the cultivation of a proper worldview, a positive outlook on life, and a strong sense of values.

China has worked to educate people through excellent cultural works. While pursuing Chinese modernization, the country places emphasis on nourishing the roots and forging the soul of our nation with advanced socialist culture, revolutionary culture, and fine traditional Chinese culture, all the while promoting socialist cultural-ethical progress through the creative transformation and innovative development of traditional Chinese culture. In recent years, we have carried out the Chinese Civilization Origins Project and the Chinese Cultural Resource Survey Project. A large number of innovative works have been created, such as the dance show "Night Banquet in Tang Dynasty Palace" and the TV show "China in the Classics," sparking widespread enthusiasm toward traditional Chinese culture. China has become the world's largest producer of books, TV plays, and animations. China's film market consistently sets new records, boasting the largest number of screens and leading box office revenues globally, presenting a number of major works such as Making a New China, The Battle at Lake Changjin, and The Age of Awakening. China has made remarkable strides in cultural progress, overcoming plateaus to reach new peaks.

China has emphasized institution building in the process of cultural advancement. In the pursuit of Chinese modernization, the country has established a framework to raise cultural-ethical standards through "Cities, Towns, Villages, Organizations, Families, and Schools of Civility." We have built centers for promoting ethical and cultural advancement in the new era, launched initiatives to raise the public's cultural-ethical standards, and worked to see that all areas of social development are imbued with core socialist values and that they become part of people's thinking and behavior. Volunteer service is an important indicator of social progress. Over the past decade, the number of registered volunteers in China increased from 2.92 million in 2012 to 232 million[①] in 2023, and community volunteer services amounted to 1.57 billion hours in duration from 2022 to 2023. In Hengyang, Hunan Province, there are nearly 1.5 million registered volunteers, about one fifth of the city's total population. They just show up where there is a need, demonstrating the vitality of Chinese volunteer services.

When the people have ideals, their country will have strength, and their nation will have a bright future. The fundamental reason why China can overcome challenges and achieve continuous and steady progress in its modernization endeavors is that the CPC has united and led all Chinese people to move forward with the utmost synergy and unity.

3) Improving China's cultural soft power

In pursuing Chinese modernization, we draw on the outstanding achievements of human civilization and apply them in innovative ways. We have integrated the basic tenets of Marxism with China's specific realities and fine traditional culture. We encourage the creative transformation and innovative development of traditional culture as we strive to develop advanced socialist culture. The comprehensive advancement of our society is a testament to the systemic and coordinated nature of Chinese modernization.

China has always emphasized the protection and preservation of cultural heritage, diligently organizing archeological excavations and documenting and interpreting their findings, to unleash all aspects of the value of our culture and cultural heritage. TV programs such as "The Nation's Greatest Treasure" and "Chinese Archaeology Assembly" have received high viewership ratings

---

① Blue Paper on Volunteer Services: Report on the Development of China's Volunteer Services (2022-2023), National Institute of Social Development, Chinese Academy of Social Sciences, and the Research Center of China's Volunteer Services.

and sparked widespread discussion among the public, inspiring the people's confidence in our culture. We strive to develop a framework for the disciplines, academia, and discourse in philosophy and the social sciences with distinctive Chinese quality, style, and ethos. Based on the lives of ordinary people, Chinese artists have created a large number of excellent works that reflect contemporary Chinese people's work and life. Some of them are even popular overseas.

4. Modernization of Harmony Between Humanity and Nature

Chinese modernization epitomizes green development. China is committed to sustainable development and coordinated economic, social, and ecological advancement. Acting on the principles of prioritizing resource conservation and environmental protection and letting nature restore itself, we pursue a model of sound development featuring improved production, higher living standards, and healthy ecosystems to ensure the sustainable development of the Chinese nation. History and today's reality have repeatedly shown that nature provides the basic conditions for human survival and development; only by observing the laws of nature can humankind avoid costly blunders arising from its exploitation. In pursuing Chinese modernization, we must respect, adapt to, and protect nature. We must act on the principle that lucid waters and lush mountains are invaluable assets and maintain harmony between humanity and nature.

1) "Lucid waters and lush mountains are invaluable assets."

This is an important concept for development and a major principle for advancing Chinese modernization. It reveals the truth that to protect the environment is to protect the productive forces, and to improve the environment is to boost the productive forces. A healthy environment represents the most equitable public good and the universal wellbeing for everyone. This has become the widely embraced consensus and incentive for conscious action throughout Chinese society.

Focusing on solving the major environmental problems harming people's health, the Chinese government has made greater efforts to keep skies blue, waters clear, and lands clean in recent years. Local governments along the Yangtze River work together to promote well-coordinated environmental conservation while avoiding excessive development in the Yangtze River basin. The water quality of the river mainstream has remained stable at Grade II for recent years. This environmental protection endeavor covers 11 provincial-level regions in China, benefiting over 40% of the Chinese population.

China has drawn redlines for the protection of ecologically significant or vulnerable areas, as well as regions with substantial ecological potential, in order to protect vital ecological spaces. Over 30% of China's total land has been designated under ecological conservation redlines. The ratio of days with good to excellent air quality in cities at and above prefecture level was 86.8%, and the days with heavy pollution decreased to 1.1% in 2023. China has become the country with the fastest rate of improvement in air quality in the world. Guangyang Island in Chongqing is the largest island in the upper reaches of the Yangtze River. After putting an end to real estate development and implementing ecological restoration in adherence to the principle of promoting well-coordinated environmental conservation and avoiding excessive development, it is now adorned with lush greenery, delightful birdsong, and babbling streams, becoming a popular ecotourism destination along the Yangtze River.

2) Taking a holistic and systematic approach to the conservation and improvement of mountains, waters, forests, farmlands, grasslands, and deserts

China is committed to green development. We have designated redlines for ecological conservation, set benchmarks for environmental quality, and imposed caps on resource utilization, all of which are being strictly observed. China is developing a system of protected areas with national parks as the mainstay, supported by nature reserves, and supplemented by nature parks, in an effort to strengthen biodiversity conservation. The first five national parks, Sanjiangyuan National Park, Wuyi Mountain National Park, Giant Panda National Park, Northeast China Tiger and Leopard National Park, and Hainan Tropical Rainforest National Park, as well as nearly 10,000 protected areas of various types at different levels have already been established. This new system of protected areas has provided effective protection for 90% of terrestrial ecosystem types, 65% of higher plant communities, and 74% of key state-protected wildlife species. It has also contributed to the increase in population numbers of over 300 rare endangered species of wild fauna and flora. The Dianchi Lake in Yunnan, with a drainage area of 2,920 square kilometers, is the largest lake in Southwestern China[①]. After persistent and dedicated input and efforts in environmental governance over decades, its water quality has improved from lower than Grade V to Grade IV, with some areas even reaching Grade III.

3) Developing an eco-friendly growth model and way of life

With concerted efforts to cut carbon emissions, reduce pollution, expand green development, and pursue economic growth, China is exploring a new approach to modernization characterized by harmony between humanity and nature, which prioritizes ecological protection, efficient and intensive use of resources, and green and low-carbon development.

China is changing rapidly every day. To make way for an ecological corridor along the Erhai Lake in Dali, Yunnan Province, various lakeside inns and bed and breakfast have been demolished. The once dusty mining areas in Anshan City,

---

[①] Reply to the No. 141370 suggestion proposed at the first session of the 14th Kunming Municipal Committee of the Chinese People's Political Consultative Conference, Kunming municipal water supply bureau, May 30, 2022 https://shuiwu.km.gov.cn/c/2022-05-30/4603910.shtml.

Liaoning Province, have transformed into green ecological gardens. A group of comparison satellite photos capturing the changes in China drew widespread attention on overseas social media in March 2023. Such massive changes in China fully demonstrate the vigor and vitality of Chinese modernization. Overseas netizens expressed awe at the remarkable achievements of China over the past decade, affirming that these changes were indeed significant and deserving of admiration.

Green development cannot be achieved without green energy. China has advanced the energy revolution, promoted clean and efficient use of coal, and speeded up the planning and development of a new system of energy sources. In the desert, thousands of solar panels glister under the sun, and at sea, large wind turbines stand tall. The six mega-cascade hydropower stations on the mainstream of the Yangtze River make up the world's largest "clean energy corridor." In 2023, clean energy consumption, including natural gas, hydropower, nuclear power, wind power and solar power, accounted for 26.4% of the total energy consumption.[1]

Chinese modernization aims to promote green and low-carbon ways of production and life by adjusting and improving the structure of the industrial, energy, and transportation sectors, pursuing high-quality development with the support of a healthy environment. As a responsible major country, China upholds the concept that humanity and nature make up a community of life, and pledges to peak carbon emissions before 2030 and reach carbon neutrality by 2060. Based on China's energy and resource endowment, we will strive to realize a transition from carbon peaking to carbon neutrality in the shortest timeframe in the world.

---

[1] The Statistical Communiqué of the People's Republic of China on the 2023 National Economic and Social Development, the National Bureau of Statistics, February 29, 2024.

4) Transcending anthropocentrism and upholding that humanity and nature make up a community of life

Since the advent of modern times, Western modernization, with its focus on capital and pursuit of maximum profits, has regarded nature as a material source solely for human exploitation, resulting in severe environmental crisis and issues. As Western countries push developing countries to copy their modernization model and shoulder the industrial costs, this model, achieved at the expense of environment, has spread to the countries of the Global South, increasingly worsening global eco-environmental issues.

Chinese modernization aims to promote harmony between humanity and nature. This concept looks beyond the Western anthropocentrism that prioritizes human interests above those of the natural world. It is rooted in China's fine traditional culture such as the ideas that "Man is an integral part of nature," "Dao follows the laws of nature," and "Take with moderation, use with prudence." We emphasize that humanity and nature make up a community of life and uphold the principles of prioritizing resource conservation and environmental protection and letting nature restore itself. We call on people to respect, adapt to, and protect nature, value and care for the environment as much as we value our own lives, and restore the serenity, harmony, and beauty of nature.

Through scientific coordination of various factors within the natural environment and human society, Chinese modernization has pioneered a new approach to achieving coordinated progress in eco-social development and environmental protection. Meanwhile, it also contributes China's wisdom and strength to jointly promoting global eco-environmental advancement and building a community of all life on Earth.

5. Modernization of Peaceful Development

In accordance with the overarching strategy of national rejuvenation and the overall context of once-in-a-century world change, Chinese Communists hold high the banner of peace, development, cooperation, and mutual benefit, champion the common values of humanity, promote the development of a human community with a shared future, and remain committed to peaceful development on the path to modernization.

1) Striving to safeguard world peace and development while pursuing our own development.

Having endured a tragic history of aggression and humiliation by Western powers, the Chinese nation deeply appreciates the value of peace. In pursuing modernization, China will not tread the old path of colonization and plunder taken by some countries, nor will it ever seek hegemony as it grows in power. China steadfastly upholds peaceful development in the pursuit of modernization. China is firm in safeguarding the international system with the United Nations at its core, the international order underpinned by international law, and the basic norms governing international relations based on the purposes and principles of the UN Charter. China advocates addressing the complex and intertwined security challenges with a spirit of solidarity and a win-win mindset, and contributes to a security architecture featuring fairness, justice, joint contribution and shared benefits. China is the only country in the world that has enshrined "keeping to a path of peaceful development" in its constitution. It now ranks first among the permanent members of the UN Security Council in terms of the number of peacekeepers dispatched. China is the only nuclear-armed country in the world that pledges never to use nuclear weapons first. In view of the future of humanity, the CPC has pioneered a path to modernization that challenges the conventional notion that a rising power is bound to seek hegemony.

Unity amid diversity is a defining feature of Chinese culture. There still exits ancient temples that combine the elements of Confucianism, Buddhism, and Daoism, or Taoism, in Hengyang, Hunan Province and Tai'an, Shandong Province, as well as various other regions of China. Many ideas from Confucianism, Buddhism, and Taoism in China, such as Confucianism's principles of benevolence, righteousness, propriety, wisdom, and faithfulness, Buddhism's emphasis on compassion and good deeds, and Daoism belief in following the laws of nature and the principle of non-action of the Great Way, harmoniously coexist and mutually complement without conflicting or opposing each other.

Based on the pluralistic unity of Chinese culture, we advocate the ideas of acting in good faith, being friendly to others, and fostering neighborliness. We have integrated the vision of a human community with a shared future with the Chinese traditional view of peace among all nations. Drawing inspiration from the notion of inclusivity embodied in the Chinese saying that "the vast ocean admits all rivers," we advocate that global affairs should be governed by all nations jointly. Recognizing that the beauty of harmony lies in diversity, we uphold that different civilizations should communicate and learn from one another to achieve common progress. Believing that we are not alone on the Great Way and the whole world is one family, we call on all countries to collaborate and unite to build a better home planet for all humanity. Chinese people reject zero-sum thinking and firmly believe in and follow the notion that cooperation leads to mutual benefits, while confrontation does no good to anyone.

The Chinese nation does not carry aggressive or hegemonic traits in its genes. Influenced by a culture of peace and harmony, China laid out the ancient Silk Road more than 2,000 years ago, promoting exchanges and development of countries along the route. More than 600 years ago, Zheng He, an esteemed navigator during the Ming dynasty, commanded the strongest fleet in the world at the time and made multiple expeditions in the Pacific and Indian oceans, visiting over 30 countries and regions across Asia and Africa. During his voyages, he did not engage in any acts of territorial conquest or aggression, but rather advocated for peace and friendship.

China works to see that multilateral institutions, such as the WTO and APEC, play their roles more effectively, cooperation mechanisms such as the G20, BRICS and Shanghai Cooperation Organization exert greater influence, and emerging markets and developing countries are better represented and have greater say in global affairs. China has successfully facilitated the restoration of diplomatic relations between Saudi Arabia and Iran, thereby mitigating the tensions between the two countries and fostering peace and stability in the Middle East. In response to the Ukrainian crisis, China maintains an objective and neutral stance, formulating its position and policies based on the merits of the situation. China is dedicated to promoting dialogue and negotiation.

2) Making greater contributions to world peace and development through our own development.

Chinese modernization is the modernization of opening the door to the world. We uphold a path of mutual benefit to promote global development. China plays an active part in the reform and development of the global governance system. We uphold true multilateralism, strive to promote trade liberalization and investment facilitation, and boost international macroeconomic policy coordination. China is committed to working with other countries to foster an international environment conducive to development and create new drivers for global growth. We work to narrow the North-South gap and assist other developing countries in accelerating development.

China put forward the initiative of jointly building the Silk Road Economic Belt and the 21st-century Maritime Silk Road (BRI) in 2013. According to *The Belt and Road Initiative: A Key Pillar of Human Community with a Shared Future* published in October 2023, over the past decade, China had signed more than 200 BRI cooperation agreements with over 150 countries and more than 30 international organizations following the principle of achieving shared growth through discussion and collaboration, launching a large number of landmark projects and small yet smart projects that benefit the people. Moreover, by that point we had consecutively held six China International Import Expo events, ten China International Fair for Trade in Services events, and three China International Consumer Products Expo events. Through these activities, China shares Chinese market and opportunities with the rest of the world.

The Regional Comprehensive Economic Partnership (RCEP) agreement came into effect on January 1, 2022. Signed by 15 countries including China, this free trade area boasts the largest population, the largest economic and trade scale, and the greatest development potential in the world. Against the backdrop of an increasing backlash against globalization and a sluggish global economic recovery, the RCEP continues to unleash policy dividends, becoming the biggest highlight in world economic growth. In 2023, China's trade with the other 14 RCEP members reached a value of 12.6 trillion yuan, indicating a growth rate of 5.3%[①] compared with 2021. "Amid declining global openness, rising trade costs, and emerging supply chain bottlenecks, the RCEP is contributing to global economic development," said Rebeca Grynspan, secretary-general of the United Nations Conference on Trade and Development. China is playing an increasingly important role in promoting global openness and cooperation and safeguarding the multilateral trading system.

The CPC believes that in the pursuit of modernization, it is imperative for every country to uphold the principles of unity, cooperation and common development and embark on a path of joint contributions, shared benefits, and win-win outcomes. As Xi Jinping said, "Countries that take the lead should make sincere efforts to help other countries develop. Blowing out other's lights does not make yours brighter; standing in someone else's way won't get you any further."

---

① Press conference of the State Council Information Office on China's 2023 imports and exports, January 12, 2024.

Chapter Four

Chinese Modernization: A New Form of Human Advancement

Chinese modernization is deeply rooted in fine traditional Chinese culture and reflects the advanced nature of scientific socialism. It draws inspiration from all of human civilization's outstanding achievements, represents the direction of human progress, and creates a new model that is different from that of Western modernization. It is a new form of human advancement.[①]

—Xi Jinping

Referring to the state of a progressing human society, civilization did not exist from the beginning, nor does it remain unchanged. Rather, it has

---

[①] "Xi Jinping addresses the opening of a study session at the Party school of the CPC Central Committee," Xinhua News Agency, February 7, 2023.

gradually evolved, upgraded, grown, and spread as driven by the development of productivity. Modern civilization is the highest achievement of social progress thus far, bringing about radical changes to the world throughout history. However, this does not mean that human civilization has reached its ideal end.

Social systems are the product of the development of civilization and also the foundation for its changes and refinement. Though the capitalist system "has created more massive and more colossal productive forces than have all preceding generations together,[①]" it has not solved the various problems of social development. In today's world, as various challenges and crises are intertwined and the development gap widens, we once again come to a historical crossroads in our pursuit of modernization.

In order to completely change the future of the nation and find a better social system for humanity, the CPC has led the Chinese people in pioneering a Chinese path to modernization and creating a new form of human advancement through a century-long struggle. With continuous improvement of theory and deepening of practice, this form of socialist civilization with Chinese characteristics has fully displayed distinctive features, remarkable advantages, and global influence as a new type of modern civilization.

1. A New Form of Values: Putting the People First

Values are the soul of any civilization and determine both its evolution process and ultimate direction. The essential difference between Chinese modernization and Western modernization in terms of value orientation is that Chinese modernization puts the people first while rejecting capital supremacy.

Capital supremacy is the fundamental value of capitalist civilization. Western

---

① "Manifesto of the Communist Party," co-authored by Karl Heinrich Marx and Friedrich Engels and translated by Chen Wangdao, Hunan People's Press, 2021.

modernization is centered on, driven by, and stuck in capital. While bringing about rapidly increasing productivity and a newfound abundance and variety of goods that have improved people's lives, Western modernization has also led to the unavoidable evils such as the expansion of materialism and the polarization between the rich and the poor.

In pursuing Chinese modernization, realizing people's aspirations for a better life has been taken as the starting point, and realizing the full and free development of every individual has been made the ultimate goal. In this way, Chinese modernization has fundamentally surpassed Western modernization in terms of the starting values formed.

1) Taking meeting the people's aspirations for a better life as the starting point of all endeavors

"Our goal is to satisfy the people's aspirations for a better life," said Xi Jinping, when he met with journalists from home and abroad in the Great Hall of the People in Beijing on November 15, 2012 after he was elected General Secretary of the CPC Central Committee. He used a simple and vivid sentence to best interpret the CPC's governance philosophy and values, which focus on putting the people first.

The purpose of Chinese modernization is to improve people's lives—it's not modernization for modernization's sake. China has always upheld people-centeric views toward its modernization drive and strived to better respond to the people's concerns and meet their needs. In doing so, it pays more attention to the people's happiness and wellbeing than can be reflected by indicators and data on paper. This has helped to avoid both deviation from the right path and path dependence, both flaws that occurred during the earlier process of modernization.

2) Taking the full and free development of every individual as the ultimate goal

With regard to the form of values, the essence of Chinese modernization is the modernization regarding the people, not materials. It strives for the people's full modernization, not their partial modernization.

Chinese modernization strives to improve both people's competency and their quality of life. For one thing, we have worked faster to build a large, high-quality modern workforce that is well-structured and well-distributed, in order to support Chinese modernization with high-quality development of the population. Another point is we have coordinated material and cultural-ethical advancement, so as to reach towering heights not only with the many skyscrapers across our great country, but also through our cultural achievements.

3) Taking whether development results benefit all people as a criterion

Common prosperity for all is an essential part of Chinese modernization.

In contrast to Western modernization, which stimulates polarization between the rich and the poor, Chinese modernization aims to achieve not only wealth, but also common prosperity for all. It is a modernization that involves everyone, not just a few. China has taken effective measures to make sure that modernization benefits all people more fairly by eliminating poverty, revitalizing rural areas across the board, building demonstration areas for achieving common prosperity, and enhancing targeted assistance and cooperation between more developed eastern and less developed western regions.

China has made a tremendous achievement unprecedented in the history of human social development by winning the battle against poverty in its pursuit of modernization. This has freed China, once a poor and weak eastern country, from absolute poverty, lifting a big country with one-fifth of the world's population out of absolute poverty. China has become the world's second largest economy with its GDP surpassing 100 trillion yuan and its per capita GDP exceeding 10,000 US dollars. With this, China, once in a marginal and backward position in the world economic system after the advent of modern times, is now contributing greatly to the world economy through its own development, thus greatly elevating the economic status of developing countries.

As a big developing country with a large-scale population, China's modernization will greatly change the world modernization landscape and stand as a positive development model among the changes unseen in a century. For a long time, America, Western European countries, and capitalist countries deeply influenced by American and European cultures have been seen as an embodiment of modernization and advancement, while developing countries have been regarded as the symbol of entrenched tradition and backwardness. Some Western countries have formed a sense of innate superiority and a hegemonic mindset that looks down upon non-Western countries and nations, leading to the prevailing of Western-centrism. The great success of Chinese modernization has challenged the superiority and arrogance of Western countries, and greatly boosted the international status, voice, and influence of developing countries.

2. A New Form of System: Constant Improvement and Reform

In the 1990s, the world socialist movement encountered serious difficulties with the disintegration of the Soviet Union and the drastic changes in Eastern European countries. The "end of history" theory stirred discussion for a time, and the social system of Western developed, capitalist countries was defined as "the end point of mankind's ideological evolution"[1] and "the final form of human government.[2]" Entering the 21st century, the rapid rise of socialist China has enabled scientific socialism to shine with renewed vigor. Chinese modernization has an advantage over Western modernization. It has proved

---

[1] *The End of History and the Last Man*, authored by Francis Fukuyama and translated by Chen Gaohua, Guangxi Normal University Press, 2016.

[2] *The End of History and the Last Man*, authored by Francis Fukuyama and translated by Chen Gaohua, Guangxi Normal University Press, 2016.

the "end of history" theory to be false by constantly improving its system and making innovations.

1) A system with a core leadership force

More than 70 years have passed since the founding of the People's Republic of China, and the Chinese nation has undergone a tremendous transformation: it has stood up, grown rich, and become stronger. This is fundamentally attributable to the CPC leading the people in establishing and improving a socialist system with Chinese characteristics.

"To understand China today, one must learn to understand the CPC." The most essential trait of Chinese socialism is the leadership of the CPC, which is also the fundamental leadership system of China.

In advancing Chinese modernization, the CPC has deepened its understanding of the laws that underlie governance by a communist party, the development of socialism, and the evolution of human society. It has remained committed to self-reform, and integrated its self-development with China's modernization drive. It has worked with energy and drive to ensure its firm and continuous leadership over China's modernization drive.

The system of CPC-led multiparty cooperation and political consultation is referred to as a new type of political party system. It is capable of representing broad interests, reflecting consistency of shared goals, promoting the sound formulation and implementation of policies, and ensuring the effectiveness of national governance. This system avoids problems such as disputes between parties, favoritism toward certain interest groups, and manipulation by a minority of political "elites."

2) A system guided by sound theory

Guided by Marxism, the system of socialism with Chinese characteristics has developed under the real conditions and culture in China, enjoying the full support of the people. Marxism has distinctive, practical character. It is not only committed to explaining the world in a rational way, but also to changing the world actively.

Over the past century, proceeding with its founding mission, the CPC has continued to produce new theories while integrating the basic tenets of Marxism with China's specific realities and fine traditional culture, thus maintaining its vigor.

From Mao Zedong Thought, Deng Xiaoping Theory, the Theory of Three Represents, the Scientific Outlook on Development, and Xi Jinping Thought on Socialism with Chinese Characteristics for a New Era, the CPC has stayed committed to integrating the basic tenets of Marxism with China's specific realities and fine traditional culture in the efforts to adapt Marxism to the Chinese context and the needs of the times, through which a guide to action can be established for its modernization drive.

In response to the questions of "what Chinese modernization is," and "how to advance it," the CPC have continued to write new chapters on the miracle of successfully advancing modernization by following the socialist path. During this process, they have produced the theory of Chinese modernization boasting rich contents, and expounded upon the central task, core content, Chinese features, essential requirements, strategic arrangements, general goals, main objectives, and major principles of Chinese modernization. The theory has elevated the understanding of past practical experience of the modernization drive and represented original development of theories on socialist modernization.

3) A system that constantly applies the achievements of civilization

China does not imitate the political systems of other countries, but it is willing to learn from other countries' beneficial governing experience. During the period of socialist construction, China drew beneficial lessons from the Soviet Union in establishing its state system and national governance system. Ever since the launch of reform and opening up, China has further opened to the outside and integrated socialism with the market economy.

At the beginning of reform and opening up, some people in China with dogmatic thinking believed the market economy was opposite to socialism. While focusing reform on balancing the relations of production, China has continued to reform its economic operation mechanism and ownership structure to establish a new economic structure, under which public ownership is the mainstay and diverse forms of ownership develop side by side, so that all forms of ownership complement and reinforce each other for common development. This helps exert the advantages of socialism while also giving play to the strengths of the market economy. This solves the question of how to integrate socialism with the market economy, which is one of the most difficult questions in world economic history.

Since the 18th CPC National Congress in 2012, China has made greater efforts in integrating socialism with the market economy in order to give full play to both sides. By exerting the role of both an "effective market" and a "capable government," China has greatly liberated and developed productive forces and greatly stimulated social vitality.

3. A New Form of Development: Becoming More Comprehensive and Coordinated

Civilization is comprised of all tangible and intangible achievements made by humans as they work to understand and change the world. A civilization must pursue progress if it is to grow, and to achieve progress it must pursue comprehensive and coordinated development. Chinese modernization is distinctly different from Western modernization in that it has rejected the one-dimensional approach that leads to alienation, instead, pursuing comprehensive and coordinated development.

1) Working toward the modernization of the people

When taking a broad perspective on civilization, material culture is the most basic level that is always a guiding factor. However, under the logic of capitalism, the "one-dimensional" pursuit of material wealth has not only caused a slew of social issues, but has also intensified alienation. Modern civilization has brought a lot to mankind, but it has also caused mankind to lose a lot.

In 1964, American scholar Herbert Marcuse published a book titled *One-Dimensional Man*, noting that the United States, as an advanced industrial society, is not a truly free and open society, but a one-dimensional society. It bribes the people with consumption and enjoyment, plunging them into a comfortable "unfreedom". According to Marcuse's sharp criticism of modern capitalist society based on his in-depth studies, in an advanced capitalist society that has become richer, alienation, instead of disappearing, has permeated more deeply, widely, and subtly into all aspects of life. Commodity fetishism dominates the economy, politics, and culture. People living in this kind of society are one-dimensional humans who have lost true freedom.

Chinese modernization, however, has targeted the modernization of its people since the very beginning in an effort to explore an approach to comprehensive and coordinated development.

2) A pattern of comprehensive and coordinated development taking shape

Material scarcity is not socialism, nor is cultural backwardness. China has developed a pattern of comprehensive and coordinated development by pursuing material, political, cultural-ethical, social, and ecological advancement, building on its previous efforts to pursue material and cultural-ethical advancement.

In as early as 1982, a strategic goal for China's modernization drive was set at the 12th CPC National Congress, stressing the necessity of pursuing high-level socialist cultural-ethical advancement while pursuing high-level material advancement. In 2012, the Five-Sphere Integrated Plan was introduced in the report to the 18th CPC National Congress, which aims to promote integrated economic, political, cultural, social, and ecological advancement. The plan regards economic advancement as the fundamental task, political advancement as the guarantee, cultural advancement as the soul, social advancement as the precondition, and ecological advancement as the foundation. In accordance with this plan we have promoted collaboration between these different spheres to advance Chinese modernization in a coordinated way. Ten years of endeavor have led to fruitful achievements. China has written a new chapter in the history of human civilization and brought human civilization to a new stage of development.

3) Making coordinated advances with a focus on addressing imbalances and inadequacies in development

In 2017, the report to the 19th National Congress of the CPC clearly stated that the principal contradiction facing Chinese society has become the contradiction between imbalanced and inadequate development and the people's ever-growing needs for a better life. Facing this all-encompassing historic change, the CPC has implemented a people-centered philosophy of development and worked to meet the people's ever-growing needs in the fields of economy, politics, culture, society, and environment by increasing the quality and efficiency of development and striving to resolve imbalances and inadequacies therein.

With its notable material advancement, steady political advancement, impressive cultural advancement, innovative social advancement, and prominent ecological advancement, China has made new progress in promoting comprehensive and coordinated development over the past decade of the new era.

Modernization is a complex system. The further it develops, the more it displays its systematic characteristics, and the more it calls for overall coordination. Following the Five-Sphere Integrated Plan, the Chinese people's multi-level needs for a better life have been fully and dynamically understood. By identifying and continuing to resolve the most practical problems that are of the greatest and most direct concern to the people, we have ensured a more complete and lasting sense of fulfillment, happiness, and security for our people.

4. A New Form of Democracy: Whole-process People's Democracy

Democracy is a political system under which the majority of people enjoy the rights granted by the state, which essentially requires that the people run the country. It is an effective means of governance in modern society. However, the term "democracy" has been co-opted by the West, leading to Western dominance in democracy narratives worldwide. In the eyes of most people in the West, the model of democracy is the Western multi-party system and universal suffrage, but for the Chinese people, this is only a form of democracy which has nothing to do with substantive democracy. The biggest difference between Chinese modernization and Western modernization in terms of governance mechanisms is that the former transcends democracy in form to promote whole-process people's democracy.

1) Democracy is for solving problems

Taking a look at the world, we can see that some countries who call their democracy "global models" have failed to govern effectively and are undergoing severe social division. On the other hand, some developing countries that have blindly copied the Western model of democracy are facing such a dilemma that there is only democracy in name but no governance.

As time has passed, people no longer take Western-centrism for granted as the standard when considering a model of democracy. Governance efficiency, rather than procedures, has gradually become a high priority criterion for assessing the performance of a democracy. Democracy is not an ornament to be used for decoration. It should be used to solve problems for the people.

According to the logic of the CPC, "substantive democracy," in which the people run the country, represents the true values of democracy. And the development of "whole-process democracy," through which the people can enjoy the benefits of peaceful development and live a happy life, reflects the efficiency of democracy.

2) Extensive, genuine, and effective democracy

The core of people's democracy in China is to uphold the unity between CPC leadership, the running of the country by the people, and law-based governance. By upholding CPC leadership, we have answered the question of who can bring the people together. By upholding the running of the country by the people, we have answered the question of what the goals of democracy are. By upholding law-based governance, we have answered the question of how to govern the country.

The underlying mechanisms of whole-process people's democracy are as follows: the people form an organic whole under the leadership of the CPC; the common will of the Party and the people is expressed in the form of the Constitution and the law; the state is organized, run, and developed on the basis of the Constitution; and the exercise of power must be within the framework of the rule of law. Finally, the people, with the CPC at the core, participate in various ways in the management of state, economic, cultural, and social affairs in accordance with the law. The Constitution and the law together with their implementation must effectively reflect the people's will, safeguard their rights and interests, and stimulate their creativity.

3) Breaking the "vote-only" model to safeguard the people's rights

Whole-process people's democracy is a basic feature of Chinese democracy, which means that democracy must be reflected in every aspect of the operation of the state apparatus, not just in the voting process. This form of democracy breaks the "vote-only" model and safeguards the people's rights to participate in democratic elections, consultations, decision-making, administration, and oversight, covering every aspect of state and social life.

Beat Schneider, professor emeritus at Bern University of the Arts in Switzerland, observed that the Chinese democratic system, as he is familiar with, has democratic institutions and people's congresses at various levels. The CPC not only maintains close ties with the people, but also unites together with them.

Chapter Four   Chinese Modernization: A New Form of Human Advancement

This is an advantage compared to the elections held every four years in Western countries.

In July 2020, the Harvard Kennedy School of Government released a report titled "Understanding CCP Resilience: Surveying Chinese Public Opinion Through Time," which shows that since 2003, there has been a notable increase in satisfaction among Chinese citizens regarding the government, with over 90% expressing satisfaction with the CPC[①]. They rated the government as more capable and effective than ever before based on indicators from the impact of national policies to the conduct of local officials.

4) Building broad consensus to make governance more effective

The reason why whole-process people's democracy works best is that its ethos, institutions, and mechanisms permeate China's political system and governance practices. Whole-process people's democracy represents the people's general will, involves the widest range of people, and extensively gathers their opinions. Being constantly improved on a regular basis, democratic consultation represents an effective way of finding the largest common ground that reflects the wishes and demands of the whole of society. Based on a wide range of participants, a consensus can be reached, providing the impetus for effective governance.

Whole-process people's democracy exists in every link of democracy. Its mechanism fills the gaps in governance and its quality ensures holistic governance. In order to improve the effectiveness of national governance, it is essential that we uphold whole-process people's democracy to better serve the people's public interests, whereby we rely on the people's strengths and wisdom to ensure national

---

① "Understanding CCP Resilience: Surveying Chinese Public Opinion Through Time", July, 2020, https://ash.harvard.edu/publications/understanding-ccp-resilience-surveying-chinese-public-opinion-through-time.

governance better reflects their will and safeguards their rights and interests.

5. A New Form of Culture: Continually Learning From the Past to Make Innovations

Culture is the lifeblood of a nation, and it gives the people a sense of belonging. Cultural confidence represents a fundamental and profound force that sustains the development of a country and a nation. With contemporary value being steeped in it, fine traditional culture, through creative transformation and innovative development, is capable of unleashing huge energy that adapts to contemporary culture and modern society. In terms of cultural identity, Chinese modernization is distinctly different from Western modernization in that it never severs ties with tradition and always learns from the past to make innovations.

1) Safeguarding cultural roots to pass on the torch of civilization

China's fine traditional culture is extensive and profound. It is the crystallization and essence of Chinese civilization, the root and soul of the Chinese nation, and the foundation upon which China can stand firm amidst strong global cultural interaction. In pursuing Chinese modernization, we have held a broad perspective on history, analyzed the mechanisms of evolution, and explored the patterns of history by taking into account historical experiences, contemporary trends, and global changes, thus putting forward strategies and measures in response to changing times.

According to some views of classical Western modernization theory, tradition and modernity are polar opposites of each other and mutually exclusive, with tradition inevitably hindering modernization, and advancing modernization inevitably denying and abandoning tradition. There are also views that deny the difference in the historical process between different countries and consider the process of advancing modernization in different countries as the constant repetition of the Western model of modernization.

Chapter Four Chinese Modernization: A New Form of Human Advancement

In exploring the path to modernization, China has been adept at viewing human society's history of modernization by taking stock of what has happened in ancient or modern times, at home and abroad. We have respected the laws of history and cultural traditions and based our current endeavors in the present to create the future, showing profound historical endowment that has been built on our nation's over 5,000 years of civilization. China is one of the four ancient civilizations in the world, and Chinese civilization is the only civilization that has continued to this day uninterrupted. The Chinese Civilization Origins Project and other important projects have produced evidence of one million years of humanity, ten thousand years of culture, and more than five thousand years of civilization in China. Zhang Guangzhi, the late, renowned Chinese-American paleoanthropologist, introduced the theory of continuity and fracture. He believed that Chinese culture is different from the Western culture in terms of its view of the universe and path to cultural development, with the former characterized by continuity and the latter riddled with fractures. His theory has provided us with a different perspective for re-examining the general laws of human advancement.

The development of world history has proved that a country should choose its path to modernization not only in accordance with general laws of modernization, but also in line with its own realities, such as its historical traditions, social system, development conditions, and external environment. China believes that only by drawing on historical experience and grasping the laws of history can a country take the initiative in pursuing modernization, seize the opportunity to realize historic transformations, keep pace with the times, and forge ahead with greater effort and determination.

2) Creative transformation and innovative development

Fine traditional Chinese culture carries national governance wisdom and provides profound inspiration for resolving common challenges confronting human society. In the process of modernization, China has promoted creative transformation and innovative development of its fine traditional culture, fully tapping into and expounding upon the contemporary value of relevant important concepts, including pursuing common good for all; regarding the people as the foundation of the state; governing by virtue; discarding the outdated in favor of the new; selecting officials on the basis of merit; promoting harmony between humanity and nature; ceaselessly pursuing self-improvement; embracing the world with virtue; acting in good faith and being friendly to others; and fostering neighborliness. By doing so, we have utilized our fine traditional culture as an important source of nutrition sustaining our core socialist values, and continued to integrate the essence of Marxism with the best of fine traditional Chinese culture.

China has worked to adapt Marxism to the Chinese context and the needs of the times, integrate the basic tenets of Marxism with the country's realities and fine traditional culture, and promote creative transformation and innovative development of its fine traditional culture, all in a bid to create a new, living cultural entity that combines the basic tenets of Marxism with fine traditional Chinese culture. In this process, the basic tenets of Marxism and fine traditional Chinese culture fit in with and complement each other. By combining the two, we have created a new cultural form of Chinese modernization and a new and unified living cultural entity, namely the modern civilization of the Chinese nation.

3) Coexistence, exchange, and mutual learning as equals

Civilizations become more colorful through exchange and richer through mutual learning. Cultural differences should not be a source of global conflict, but rather a driving force for human advancement. Championing equality, mutual learning, dialogue, and inclusiveness between civilizations, Chinese modernization enables cultural exchanges to transcend estrangement, mutual learning to transcend clashes, and coexistence to transcend feelings of superiority, thus helping promote civilizations along a balanced, positive and virtuous trajectory. According to Western modernization theory, the development of human society is divided into two stages—civilization and barbarism, and the world is divided into modern industrial societies and non-industrial societies. Modern industrial societies of the West are meant to be role models for the entire non-Western world, and Western civilization is the pinnacle of human advancement.

The Chinese people, however, believe that just as human beings may differ in skin color and language, civilizations may also vary in color and hue; no civilization is superior to another. Various civilizations created by human society have laid solid foundations for modernization in various countries. Chinese modernization advocates respecting the diversity of world civilizations, and upholds equality and respect while rejecting hubris and prejudice to deepen understanding of the differences between our own civilization and others when facilitating harmonious coexistence between different civilizations. Civilizations do not need to clash with each other. We should not only keep our own civilizations flexible and dynamic, but also create conditions for other civilizations to flourish. Together we can make the garden of world civilizations colorful and vibrant.

Chinese civilization has been known for its openness and inclusiveness since ancient times, and it has continued to find new life through exchanges with and learning from other civilizations. Being deeply rooted in China's fine traditional culture, Chinese modernization fully taps into and expounds upon the contemporary value of this culture and the intellectual features of Chinese civilization, embodies the advanced nature of scientific socialism, draws inspiration from all of human civilization's outstanding achievements, and represents the direction of human progress, thus creating a new model that is different from Western model of modernization. As a new form of human advancement, Chinese modernization, by drawing from other civilizations, will surely enrich the garden of world civilizations, provide theoretical inspiration for resolving common challenges confronting human society, and provide intellectual guidance for the modernization of humanity.

6. A New Form of Global Governance: Building a Human Community with a Shared Future

Peace and security, like sunshine and rain, are hardly noticed when we are benefiting from them, but without them we are lost. Facing the changing times and an increasingly turbulent world, people of all countries aspire to peace and stability. China's modernization drive aims not only to benefit the Chinese people, but also to promote the common development of the world. In other words, our goal is not only to make the country stronger and realize national rejuvenation, but also to contribute to human progress and world harmony. Chinese modernization is different from Western modernization in terms of the way it perceives global governance. It opposes unilateralism and protectionism and advocates building a community with a shared future for humanity.

1) Pursuing common values and safeguarding a shared future

A peaceful and developing world should have different forms of civilization and allow for diverse paths toward modernization. China holds dear humanity's shared values of peace, development, fairness, justice, democracy, and freedom, rejects the practice of forming small circles or playing zero-sum games, and calls for joint efforts to build a new type of international relations featuring mutual respect, fairness, justice, and mutually beneficial cooperation. By doing so, we will be able to expand the convergence of interests and achieve the greatest synergy possible.

With a confrontational zero-sum mentality, some Western countries used to rely on their "early bird" advantage in modernization to export their modernization models to other countries. They shifted the costs and crises generated by their own wealth accumulation onto developing countries through economic exploitation and colonial plunder, placing numerous obstacles to economic and social development in the path of late-comer countries pursuing modernization, thus giving rise to serious imbalances and injustices in world modernization.

China, adhering to the world view of harmony among all nations, has always been concerned with the future of humanity, striving to provide new opportunities for world development via new achievements in Chinese modernization. Following the right path of peaceful development, China has advocated bridging differences through dialogue and resolving disputes through cooperation, linking its future with that of peoples around the world to promote the building of a community with a shared future for humanity.

The Chinese people have always celebrated and strived to pursue the vision of peace, amity, and harmony. China has never invaded or bullied others in the past, and will never do so in the future, nor will it seek hegemony. China has always worked to safeguard world peace, contribute to global development, preserve international order, and provide public goods, and it will continue to provide the world with new opportunities through its new development.

2) Safeguarding common order and improving global governance

There is no such thing as a single authoritative model of modernization, nor is there a one-size-fits-all standard for modernization. In pursuing modernization, China refuses to follow the old path of war, colonization, and plunder taken by some countries. Furthermore, China is opposed to certain countries that maliciously distort the meaning of international law, package their own will as the so-called "rules-based international order," and impose it upon the international community, wantonly infringing on the legitimate rights of other countries.

China advocates a vision of global governance featuring shared growth through discussion and collaboration. We have actively participated in, promoted, and joined hands with other countries to push forward reform and development of the global governance system in a bid to make the international order fairer and more equitable. We have worked to advance the modernization of human society through continued efforts to guarantee equal rights, equal opportunities, and fair rules for all.

Chinese modernization aims to resolve the problems that have arisen from the process of modernization and that Western countries have failed to solve, such as capital-centric practices leading to the polarization between the rich and the poor, expansion of materialism, and expansion and plunder. China will stand firmly on the right side of history and on the side of human progress. Dedicated to peace, development, cooperation, and mutual benefit, we will strive to safeguard world peace and development as we pursue our own development and make greater contributions to world peace and development through our own development.

3) Fulfilling our responsibility as a major country and calling for joint action

In September 2021, China put forward Global Development Initiative, advocating a people-centered, inclusive, and innovation-driven approach and harmony between humanity and nature. China believes that all countries must join hands and cooperate with each other as their development is closely linked and their people share a common future.

From proposing the Global Development Initiative in September 2021 to proposing the Global Security Initiative in April 2022 and the Global Civilization Initiative in March 2023, Xi Jinping has provided important public goods for the international community based on his deep concern for the future of humanity and insight into the prospects of human advancement. The three initiatives put forward have each enriched and expanded the theoretical connotation and practical means of building a community with a shared future for humanity. According to Robert Lawrence Kuhn, chairman of the US-based Kuhn Foundation, the idea of a community with a shared future for humanity is a great vision for improving global governance, which shows that China is willing to take on more global responsibility for promoting world peace and

Chapter Four Chinese Modernization: A New Form of Human Advancement

prosperity[①].

Chinese modernization has expanded the channels for developing countries to achieve modernization by providing them with a brand-new option, and offered a Chinese proposal for humanity's search for a better social system. Every country's effort to independently explore the path to modernization in line with its national conditions should be respected, and developing countries have the right and the ability to independently explore their own unique paths to modernization that fit them best. We will always develop the country and the nation through our own strength and maintain a firm grasp on the future of China's development and progress. We will also respect and support the independent choices of peoples around the world regarding their own development paths, in a concerted effort to draw a new vision of the future featuring harmonious coexistence of modernization in diverse forms.

[①] "Contributing to solving common problems confronting humanity: 20th CPC National Congress in eyes of international community," Xinhua News Agency, October 27, 2022.

Conclusion

Today, our world, our times, and history itself are changing in ways like never before. A new round of scientific and technological revolution and industrial transformation is well under way. The deficit in peace, development, security, and governance is growing. The world has entered a new period of turbulence and change and has once again reached a crossroads in history. Its future will be decided by all the world's people.

If we say Western modernization is a prelude to modernization, then China and other developing countries are becoming increasingly involved in the symphony of modernization.

The history of humanity's pursuit of modernization is a history of developing the new from the old through exchanges and mutual learning between different civilizations. In the arduous struggle to pursue modernization, the Communist Party of China has led the Chinese people in pioneering a path of Chinese modernization, creating a new model for human advancement, expanding the channels for developing countries to achieve modernization, and contributing a Chinese approach to humanity's search for better social systems.

Chinese modernization is socialist modernization pursued under the leadership of the Communist Party of China. Being adept at upholding fundamental principles and breaking new ground, the Communist Party of China has integrated the basic tenets of Marxism with China's specific realities and fine traditional culture in a continued effort to adapt Marxism to the Chinese context and the needs of our times. On this basis, it has enriched scientific socialism through the bustling development and great achievements of Chinese modernization, turning the pursuit of common prosperity into concrete action and rendering the ideal of universal harmony into a form no longer beyond reach.

Advancing Chinese modernization is a trailblazing undertaking. On the journey ahead, we will inevitably be confronted with risks and challenges, difficulties and obstacles, and even dangerous storms, some of which we can foresee and others we cannot. It should be clearly noted that in today's world, hegemonism, power politics, and bullying are severely impacting world peace. Some countries are inciting division and confrontation, imposing decoupling, and disrupting industrial and supply chains, thus severely threatening global security. Regional security hotspot issues continue to emerge, regional conflicts and disturbances are frequent, traditional and non-traditional security threats are intertwined, and a backlash against globalization is rising as protectionism mounts and world economic recovery is sluggish.

Our future is bright, but we still have arduous tasks to accomplish and a long way to go. Chinese Communists would neither be complacent with what we have achieved in the past, nor would we be hesitant about moving forward in the face of external pressure. At the same time, Chinese Communists have been committed to following a modernization path of peaceful development. We firmly believe that humanity constitutes an organic whole, and the Earth is our common home. In the face of common challenges, no person or country can remain insulated. The only way out is to work together in harmony with one accord. The Chinese have believed that "all under Heaven are of one family" since ancient times. We have advocated "affinity between all people and all creatures," "peace among all nations," and "harmony under Heaven." We have aspired to create a better world in which "when the path is just, the common good will reign over all under Heaven," and we are dedicated to building a human community with a shared future.

As an ancient Chinese saying goes, "All living things grow side by side and do not impede one another. All roads run parallel and do not counter one another." Only when all countries pursue the common good, live in harmony, and engage in cooperation for mutual benefit will there be sustained prosperity and guaranteed security. China is committed to building a world of lasting peace through dialogue and consultation, a world of universal security through collaboration and shared benefits, a world of common prosperity through mutually beneficial cooperation, an open and inclusive world through exchanges and mutual learning, and a clean and beautiful world through green and low-carbon development.

We are convinced that as long as all countries work together to pursue peaceful development and mutually beneficial cooperation, champion equality, mutual learning, dialogue, and inclusiveness between civilizations, and hold dear humanity's shared values, we will definitely be able to create a better future for modernization and human advancement.

难以置信的变化

Incredible Transformation--
Chinese Modernization through
the Eyes of an American

——一个美国人眼中的中国式现代化

中国式现代化发展之路

　　《难以置信的变化——一个美国人眼中的中国式现代化》由新华社国家高端智库出品，是配合《中国式现代化发展之路》智库报告拍摄的纪录片。全片共5集，每集13分钟。摄制组历时6个多月，行程4万多公里，深入中国15个省、自治区、直辖市，采访了科技工作者、医生、教师、农民、环保工作者、非遗传承人等，以一个长期在中国生活工作的美国人的视角，讲述了中国式现代化的生动故事。现将脚本刊载，以飨读者。

　　Incredible Transformation -- Chinese Modernization through the Eyes of an American is a documentary produced by the New China Research, the think tank of Xinhua News Agency, to supplement its report Chinese Modernization: the Way Forward. It consists of 5 episodes, each lasting 13 minutes. Over a period of more than six months, the production crew traveled more than 40,000 kilometers across 15 provincial regions. They interviewed a wide range of individuals, including scientists and engineers, doctors, teachers, farmers, environmental protection personnel, and inheritors of intangible cultural heritage. Through the perspective of an American who has lived and worked in China for a long time, it vividly tells the stories unfolding in Chinese modernization. The following is the script.

难以置信的变化：一个美国人眼中的中国式现代化

新华社大型纪录片《难以置信的变化：一个美国人眼中的中国式现代化》之《第一集 润物细无声》

・中国式现代化发展之路・

第一集

润物细无声

【解说】中国，人类文明的重要发祥地之一。那么，她是如何成就今天令人难以置信的现代化，并给世界带来如此巨大变革的呢？

China, one of the birthplaces of human civilization. So how did she achieve today's incredible modernization and bring such transformation to the world?

【字幕】潘维廉厦门大学管理学院美籍教授

William N. Brown, Professor, School of Management, Xiamen University (United States)

【解说】我是潘维廉，今年 67 岁，我来自美国。35 年前，我第一次踏上这片土地，未曾料想的是，我从此再没有离开。

这是我工作了 35 年的大学，这里是我的家，这是我美丽的城市——厦门。而中国的美丽可远不止于此。

I am Bill Brown. I am 67 years old and from the U.S.. When I first set foot on this land 35 years ago, I never imagined I'd never leave. This is the university where I've worked for 35 years. This is my home. This is my beautiful city Xiamen. And China has far more beauty than this.

【字幕】难以置信的变化——一个美国人眼中的中国式现代化

Incredible Transformation—Chinese Modernization through the Eyes of an American

第一集　润物细无声

Mount To The Heart

【解说】我经常告诉我的朋友，要了解一个地方，最好的方法，就是打开你的双眼亲身去看看。

1994年，我自驾4万多公里环游中国，耗费整整三个月时间。但2019年再出发，只用了32天。

个体出行和上亿人的交通流量，不可同日而语，特别是在每年的春运期间，一个月左右的时间里，发生了30亿人次以上的出行，相当于在短时间内搬空了非洲、美洲、欧洲、大洋洲的总人口。这不再是单纯的数字概念，而反映着一个政府真正理解14亿人民复杂需求的精妙治理能力，其中包含着与人民的共情，并结合了面向未来的创建性智慧。也许可以说，对于人民的共情，最典型的体现之一就是对于生命的尊重，就让我们去探访一个发展中国家的医疗体系最难以触及的区域。也许，这样的地方能更好地体现现代化医疗的本质。

I often tell my friends that the best way to get to know a place is to use your own eyes and see it for yourself.

In 1994, I drove more than 40 thousand kilometers around China and it took us three full months. But in 2019, it only took 32 days.

But the travel of a few individuals like me is nothing compared to the transportation flood of billions of people. Especially during the Chinese New Year holiday month, Chinese make more than 3 billion trips equivalent to moving the total populations of Africa, the Americas, Europe and Oceania. This is no longer a mere statistic, but a vivid reflection of the capacity of a government that uses wisdom and empathy to understand and meet the complex needs of its 1.4 billion people. China's empathetic leadership is perhaps best seen in its respect for life. Now let's go to what we imagine is the most inaccessible area of the developing country's healthcare systems. Places like this best reflect the essence of medical modernization.

【字幕】广东珠海桂山岛

Guishan Island, Zhuhai, Guangdong

【解说】中国广东桂山岛，它地处香港、珠海、澳门之间，是各国船只通往珠江口的要地。经常受到台风侵袭。2017年的那场"天鸽"台风，是王桂湘医生，此生难忘的场景。

Guishan Island in Guangdong, China, is located between Hong Kong, Zhuhai and Macao. It is an important place for ships from all over the world to pass through and it's often hit by typhoons. In 2017, Typhoon Pigeon (Hato) struck here. It became a scene that Wang Guixiang will remember for the rest of his life.

【同期】中心风力在桂山就有17级了。白天就已经开始吹了，差不多晚上一下子整个大门都被它吹走，什么心情就说不出来了。

哪位啊？

喂？

王院长。

伤得很厉害，右手有伤，动不了了。

那个是台风打那些船玻璃刮了一个口。

我们现在去哪儿？

抢救室。

没水没电了，手持大大的电筒，我马上就帮他清创缝合。

先做心电图。

因为还在台风期间，没有船的话只会重病很重，也送不出去。

双氧水、纱布。

外面的伤口就帮你包住了，这个骨折这个地方就要到外面拍片什么才知道。

等一下要转院出去，你有没有熟人联系船？

没带钱。

钱是小事，先检查清楚。

The wind force at the typhoon's center on Guishan Island was 17. The wind started blowing during the day. Believe it or not, during the night the whole gate was blown away. I was dumbstruck by the horrible scene.

Who's speaking?

Hello?

Director Wang.

His right hand was seriously wounded.

He cannot move.

(He was hit by) glass broken by the Typhoon on the boat.

Where're we going?

The emergency room.

The water and electricity were cut off. With a large flashlight in hand, I had him cleaned and stitched up in no time.

Take an EKG first. The typhoon was still raging then, so we cannot transfer him out using a boat and his condition would worsen.

Hydrogen peroxide.

- 177 -

Gauze.

I've bound up the wound for you. As for the fracture, you'll need to take an X-ray outside the island to be diagnosed. You have to be transferred to another hospital soon.

Do you happen to know someone who can arrange a boat for you?

I didn't bring money with me. No need to worry about money. Find out the problem first.

【解说】桂山岛上只有一家卫生院，王医生是桂山岛上唯一的院长。每年夏天，在这座受南亚热带季风影响的小岛上，这样的紧张状况就是他生活的常态。曾经很长时间，令王桂湘和他的同事无奈的是，桂山因为地处偏远地区，医疗资源和医疗效率都极大受到限制。

There is only one hospital on Guishan Island and Dr. Wang is the only director. Every summer on this small island shrouded by the southern subtropical monsoon, emergencies like this are Wang's daily routine. For a long time, Wang and his colleagues had to accept that medical resources and efficiency were greatly limited in this remote island.

【同期】等到第三天有船了，他们才去进一步的处理。因为你不可能在台风那个时候，你说你帮我派一条船出去，谁敢派这个船？派不了。

It was not until the third day that a boat became available and the patient got further treatment. You see, it's impossible in the weather of typhoon to request a boat for patient transport. Nobody dared to arrange the boat.

【字幕】王桂湘珠海市人民医院鹤洲医院桂山镇中心卫生院院长

Wang Guixiang, Director of Guishan Town Central Health Center, Zhuhai City

【同期】所以这个压力就是我们医护人员。

So the pressure is on us medical workers.

【解说】灾难应急非常重要，海岛上日常的医疗救助也不容忽视。王医生自己已经到了退休年龄，但他更牵挂岛上的这些老年人。做海岛医生，就是要做岛民的全科医生。

Emergency medical care is very important on this island as is daily medical care. Dr. Wang himself has reached retirement age, but he is even more concerned about these elderly people on the island. An island doctor is literally the islander's general practitioner.

【同期】每个居民都在我们卫生院做了一个基本健康档案，所以我们每年也要跟他们做一个基本的健康体检，通知这些老人家都过来做一下，也希望我们每个医护人员都把它落实下来。

Our health center has set up for each islander a basic health record. Each year we would provide them with a basic health examination and notify all the elderly residents to come. I hope that all of our doctors and nurses here can keep it going.

【解说】一方面是一线医疗工作者最为直接的守护，一方面岛民也持续见证着卫生院硬件条件的飞速改善。如今，在5G远程医疗技术赋能之下，这座小岛已连通中国医疗信息技术与医疗服务深度融合的大潮。

Frontline medical work brings the most immediate guardianship to the islanders, while they continue to witness rapid improvements in hospital infrastructure. Today, this small island hospital is empowered by state-of-the-art 5G telemedicine technology being integrated into the wave of innovation in healthcare information technology in China.

【同期】因为我单位在这里，所以我就不能离开太远。最远是什么？不超过三五百米我就回来了。你离得太远万一有事情的话，他们找我找不到，那我的责任就很重大了。

My duty is here, so I can't be too far away. How far is that? I can't be more than 300-500 meters away from the health center. If I were not available when they need me, it would be my responsibility.

【解说】三十多年间，王桂湘也看着桂山岛从曾经的渔港转变为如今的海洋经济特色小镇，粤港澳大湾区中间的璀璨明珠。

Over the course of three decades, he has witnessed Guishan Island transforming from a former fishing port into a thriving coastal economic town, a shining pearl in the middle of the Greater Bay Area.

【字幕】2021年，中国每千人口执业医师数量3.09人，首超美国2.7人的数字。到2025年中国每千人口执业医师数达到3.2人，将接近西欧国家平均4.0人的数字。

In 2021, China had 3.09 practicing physicians per 1000 population, surpassing the U.S. figure of 2.7 for the first time. China's National Health Commission also has a clear plan to increase this number to 3.2 by 2025, gradually approaching the figure of 4.0 in Western European countries.

【解说】也正如桂山所见，中国的5G医疗正在快速度普及，为中国各地的患者提供了有效的医疗服务。让医疗保健不再受限于地域，确保了每个中国人都能从这样的中国式现代化中受益。

As we can see in Guishan, the widespread adoption of 5G healthcare in China is rapidly providing efficient medical services to patients across the country, breaking down geographical barriers to healthcare access. This ensures that everyone in China can benefit from this unique Chinese path to modernization.

【解说】"未来"，对于一个教师而言是频繁会接触的词汇。过去35年，我深刻理解了几代中国人关于教育的信条：知识改变命运。而同时，我也在不断思考教育的本质。思考教育如何彻底改变了中国无数年轻人的命运。如何改变了这个国家的命运。

而说到命运，也许在命运释放它无情的力量的地方，我们更能体会到逆转命运所带来的感动。

The word "future" is one that a teacher is frequently exposed to over the past 35 years. I've come to deeply understand the motto that generations of Chinese have firmly believed about education: KNOWLEDGE CHANGES DESTINY. I constantly think about the nature of education. I think about how education has revolutionized the destiny of countless young people in China, and changed the destiny of this country.

Speaking of destiny, it is precisely where destiny unleashes its relentless power, that we can best appreciate the moving power of reversing it.

【字幕】云南莲城镇落松地村

Luosongdi Village, Liancheng Town, Yunnan Province

【同期】我是1986年9月份来到这个地方的，我第一眼看到那些被病魔侵蚀的躯体严重畸形的那些家长，当时我非常害怕，我掉头就跑。后来那个医生就跟我说，你跑什么跑？你跑了这些孩子怎么办？

他们大的都十一二岁了，都没上过学。没人愿意来当他们的老师。

I first came here in September 1986. Seeing the people whose bodies had been severely deformed by the disease, I was terrified. I turned around and ran away. Then the doctor said to me, "How can you leave? Who will teach these children if you leave?"

The oldest of them are already 11 or 12 years old and have never been to school. No one wants to be their teacher.

【解说】落松地村地处中国西南边境省云南的偏远大山里。这里曾经是麻风病患者的集中康复地区，于是成了人见人怕的"麻风村"。1986年，农加贵来到这里，做起了乡村教师。

The village of Luosongdi is located in the remote mountains of Yunnan, a border province in southwest China. Because it used to be a centralized rehabilitation area for leprosy patients, it became a "leprosy village" that was once shunned by everyone. In 1986, Nong Jiagui came here and became a rural teacher.

【同期】在这个地方是困难非常多的。

There were numerous difficulties at that time.

【字幕】农加贵广南县莲城镇北宁中心学校落松地小学教师

Nong Jiagui, Teacher, Luosongdi Primary School, Liancheng County, Yunnan

【同期】当时不仅仅是校舍的简陋，主要是来自外面的歧视和不理解，后来我看到那些孩子们，渴求知识那种眼神，我就留下来，一干就到今天。

The school facilities were shabby. Worse still, local people were discriminated against. When I looked in the children's eyes and saw their thirst for knowledge, I decided to stay. I've been working here ever since.

【同期】床前明月光，疑是地上霜。

举头望明月，低头思故乡。

Abed I see a silver light, I wonder if it's frost on the ground.

Looking up I find the moon bright, bowing in homesickness I'm drowned.

【解说】知识的力量可以驱除误解，塑造未来，点燃勇气。

在农加贵的怀抱中，孩子们找到了梦想和信念的力量，这种涟漪效应也影响到村里的大人们。

The power of knowledge dispels misunderstandings, shapes futures and ignites courage.

In Nong's embrace, children find strength to rise to dream and to believe. It's like this ripple effect that reaches the adults too.

【同期】我从一个代课教师，转为一个公办教师以后，就把我调离了麻风村。我记得那一天，我给那几个孩子上最后一节课的时候，全班的学生没有一个人说话，只有那个班长问我"老师不走行吗？"我说"不行"。他又说"那今后你还会不会来看我们？"我说"会来。有时间我一定会来。"

然后，我就想偷偷地就想走了。没想到那一天又下着大雨，我们双方之间都可以说是分不清楚，对方到底脸上流下来是雨水还是泪水。但是孩子们一直哭着把我送到新的学校，担心以后就再也见不到我。

后来群众不断地向教育局反映情况，说一定要让我回来。所以后来我就第二个学期，我又回来，跟村民们相处到了今天。

我从1986年到今天已经是37年了。这么多年，共送走小学毕业生是12个班，126个孩子。

这126个孩子，如今有考上公务员的、有当老师的、有当医生的、有当警察的……我来到这个地方，才感受到知识真的会改变命运。

After a period of substitute teaching, I became a full-time government-paid teacher and was soon transferred out of the village. I remember that day, when I gave my last lesson to those kids, the students were all in silence. Only the class monitor asked me, "Is it okay if you don't leave us?" I said "No." Then he asked "Would you come back to see us someday?" I said "Yes. If I'm free, I'll definitely come." I added.

I planned to leave quietly. But it was raining heavily that day. We couldn't tell if it was rain or tears on each other's faces. The children sent me off to my new school in tears. They were afraid they'd never see me again.

Later, the villagers kept contacting the Education Bureau, insisting that they must let me back. So in the second semester, I came back and I've stayed here to this day.

It's been 37 years since 1986. Over the years, I witnessed the graduation of 12 elementary school classes totaling 126 children. Among them, some are now civil servants, teachers, doctors and police officers.

中国式现代化发展之路

My experience here allowed me to realize that knowledge can indeed change one's life.

【解说】过去十几年来，中国持续推进乡村教师支持计划，数以百万的乡村教师继而也将这样的支持传递到每个孩子心中。

Over the past decade, China has continued to promote a support program for rural teachers. Millions of them have in turn passed on this support to every child.

【字幕】上世纪五十年代，中国80%的人口是文盲，学龄儿童入学率只有20%。今天，文盲率降至2.67%。

In the 1950s, 80% of Chinese people were illiterates, and the enrollment rate of school-age children was only 20%. Today, the illiteracy rate has dropped to 2.67%.

【解说】这是厦门最热闹的美食街。

This is the busiest food street in Xiamen.

【同期】谢谢你

Thank you.

【解说】今天的中国，美食的意义并不仅仅是愉悦享乐。粮食安全至关重要。它帮助十多亿人摆脱贫困，走出一条独具中国特色的粮食可持续发展道路。特别是考虑到，中国必须用仅占世界9%的耕地，养活占世界20%的人口。

In China today, food is about more than just pleasure. Food security is pivotal to lifting more than a billion people out of poverty and developing a unique Chinese path to food sustainability, especially given that China must feed 20% of the world's population on only 9% of the world's arable land.

【同期】利用海南的气候，冬季去海南去繁殖。

Taking advantage of Hainan's climate, we go there in the winter to pollinate seeds.

【字幕】程相文河南省鹤壁市农业科学院名誉院长研究员

Cheng Xiangwen, Researcher, Honorary Faculty Director, Hebi City Academy of Agricultural Sciences, Henan

【同期】那儿属于热带，咱在那儿播种，可以种一次，到5月份回来再种，能加快一半时间，

Hainan belongs to a tropical area. If we go and sow the seeds once (in winter), we can come back in May and sow again. The pollination cycle will be halved.

【解说】鹤壁市农科院的农业科学专家程相文，自上世纪60年代开始，就这样跨越2000多公里，往返于中国北方城市河南鹤壁和热带岛屿海南岛。

如今他已经87岁，依然做着他从事了一生的事业——玉米育种。

Cheng Xiangwen, an agricultural expert from the Hebi City Academy Of Agricultural Sciences, has been making this journey across more than 2,000 kilometers since the 1960s. Each year, he would travel frequently between the northern Chinese city of Hebi in Henan province, and the tropical island of Hainan.

Today, he is 87 years old and still doing what he has been doing all his life—corn breeding.

【同期】粮食紧缺的时候，那品种只要高产，人吃饱就行了。下一步高产还得抗自然灾害，主要是一个抗倒、抗病。

When food was in short supply, seeds would be expected to have high yields to avoid starvation. Next, the seeds need to be resistant to the effects of natural disasters, especially collapse and disease.

【解说】海南是个"天然大温室"，是全中国最大的南方育种基地。在这里北方农作物的育种周期缩短了1/3到1/2。新中国成立以来育成的农作物新品种中70%以上都在这诞生。如今，程相文每年依旧会把海南

收获的种子带回北方播种，频繁往返。因为一粒良种，要从几千甚至上万个育种材料中筛选，会经历数不清的失败。

Hainan is a "natural greenhouse" and China's largest southern breeding base. Here, the breeding cycle of northern crops was shortened by 1/3 to 1/2. Since the founding of the People's Republic of China, more than 70% of China's new crop varieties were born here. Until today, Cheng still brings the seeds harvested in Hainan back to the north, making frequent round trips all year round. This is because a good seed must be selected from thousands or even tens of thousands of breeding materials after countless failures.

【同期】这个玉米就是我们去年前一个在海南培育的种了那是3000多棵材料先看看它的产量，看看它的好坏吧，我选种12个。

This variety of corn was bred in Hainan last year. We grew more than 3,000 plants to assess the yield and quality of the corn. I selected 12 samples for seed breeding.

【解说】8月，玉米育种材料的试验田即将进入大规模授粉期，但连续几天的大雨，让他对马上开始的授粉作业十分担忧。

In August, at the test field of corn breeding materials, a large-scale pollination period is about to begin. But after several days of heavy rain, he starts to worry about the pollination operation that will begin soon.

【同期】如果下雨的花粉呢，一般的是，下雨以后那地方一湿，这花粉就没生命力了，会减产。6000个，计划是今年最后入选100个，但是，不是成品，只能说明年再继续再看。它不是光人吃的，很多工业啥发展，没有粮食那就不行。所谓民以食为天，粮食第一。出新品种，因为只有根据人的需要。事物的发展需要，无止境。

Rain may destroy the pollen. Normally, when it rains, the wet pollen loses its fertility and the whole crop will be less productive. This year we have planted

6,000 corn plants from which 100 will be selected. But the selected plants do not necessarily produce the final seeds. We'll check their performance next year. The corn is not just for human consumption but is also required by a variety of industries. Food is the paramount necessity of the people, and it always comes first. Development of new crop varieties according to the needs of people and changing circumstances is an endless journey

【解说】如今，即使在中国最偏远的地区，曾经崎岖不平的土路，如今也变成了通往家门口的平坦水泥路。教育和医疗条件也得到了显著改善，将人口基数庞大的难题，转化为现代化发展优势。

这一切不是数字，不是新闻素材，也不是古老文化的异域风光。它们以及这个古老而充满青春活力的国家，在现代化进程中发生的一切，在人类文明历史中重新定义了现代化一词。也许可以说，这就是我选择留在这里的原因。

面对未来，还有哪里会是如此令人激动又充满愿景的梦想故事发生之地，吸引着人们希望成为其中的参与者呢！

Today, even in the most remote parts of China, the once bumpy dirt roads are now smooth concrete roads which lead right to village doorsteps and education. Medical conditions have improved dramatically, transforming what seemed a demographic challenge into a modernization and development advantage.

These are not numbers, news stories or exotic landscapes of ancient cultures They and everything else that is happening in the modernization of this ancient, but vibrantly youthful country have redefined the word modernization. Perhaps it's fair to say that that's why I've chosen to stay here.

Facing the future, where else can one dream of seeing firsthand such an exciting visionary story and even playing a small part in it.

· 中国式现代化发展之路 ·

新华社大型纪录片《难以置信的变化：一个美国人眼中的中国式现代化》之

《第二集 同欲者胜之》

第二集

同欲者胜之

【字幕】潘维廉 厦门大学管理学院美籍教授

William N. Brown, Professor, School of Management, Xiamen University (United States)

【解说】自1991年我第一次到访北京以来,这座中国的首都发生了巨大的变化。如今,她的繁华与现代化程度跟任何一个国际大都市相比毫不逊色。但对我来说,过去十年中国最显著的变化是:欠发达地区生活条件的显著改善,特别是在农村地区,政府通过精准扶贫成功消除了极端贫困。

Beijing, the capital of China, has changed so much since my first visit in 1991. Today, it is as prosperous and modern as any metropolis in the world. But for me, the most striking change in China over the past decade has been the remarkable improvement in living conditions in less developed areas, especially in rural areas where the government has succeeded in eradicating extreme poverty through precise poverty alleviation.

中国式现代化发展之路

【字幕】难以置信的变化——一个美国人眼中的中国式现代化

Incredible Transformation—Chinese Modernization through the Eyes of an American

第二集　同欲者胜之

Share in one purpose

【解说】杭州，中国东部的一线大都市。700多年前，马可·波罗说杭州是世界上最伟大的城市。

Hangzhou is a first-tier metropolis in eastern China. Over 700 years ago, Marco Polo said Hangzhou was the greatest city on earth.

【同期】它的原产地，在溪龙黄杜村，被称为"白叶一号"。

Its place of origin is Huangdu Village of the Xilong Town. It is known as "White Leaf No. 1".

【解说】而我们的故事要从距杭州80多公里外的安吉市黄杜村开始。

30多年前，贫困的黄杜村，甚至有很多人家还没通电，到1997年，当地人开始种植白茶，自此迎来了转机。

Today's story begins about 80 kilometers away from Hangzhou, in Anji City's Huangdu village.

More than 30 years ago, many homes in the impoverished village of Huangdu did not even have electricity. By 1997, the locals began to grow white tea and since then there has been a turnaround.

【同期】在1997年，我们没有种白茶之前，我们人均（年）收入还不足1000元。那么种白茶到现在已经20多年过去了，那我们现在的人均（年）收入已经超过了7万元。

In 1997, before we planted white tea here, the local annual income per capita was less than 1,000 yuan. It's been more than 20 years since we first planted white tea here and the annual income per capita has now exceeded 70,000 yuan.

【字幕】盛阿伟 黄杜村党总支书记 村委会主任

Sheng Awei, Secretary of the General Party Branch, chairman of the Village Committee, Huangdu Village, Anji, Zhejiang

【同期】2018年，我们和总书记写了一封信。我们向他汇报，我们这个村这20多年来发展得很好，真正实现了一片叶子富了一方百姓。

In 2018, we wrote a letter to General Secretary Xi Jinping, reporting to him that our village has developed well over the past 20 years and that white tea has brought prosperity to the local people.

【解说】如今，安吉白茶也成中国茶叶市场上的顶级品种。而富裕的黄杜村决心将这"黄金树叶"传递更多人手中。

Today, Anji white tea has also become a top-grade variety in the Chinese tea market. A newly prosperous Huangdu village decided to pass the "gold leave" around.

【字幕】钱义荣 安吉县溪龙乡农业农村办公室四级调研员

Qian Yirong, Researcher, Xilong Town Agriculture Rural Office, Anji, Zhejiang

【解说】钱义荣，人称"茶博士"，作为安吉的茶叶技术人员，钱义荣主动领下任务去蹲点帮扶中国其他贫困地区，位于贵州隐秘大山里的沿河土家族自治县就是其中之一。

Qian Yirong has been nicknamed "Dr. Tea". As a tea technician in Anji, Qian Yirong took the initiative to take on the task of helping other less developed areas in China. Yanhe Tujia Minorities Autonomous County located in the hidden mountains of the southwestern province of Guizhou is one of them.

中国式现代化发展之路

【同期】2018年我们从铜仁过来，都要四个多小时。路又窄又小，旁边都是悬崖峭壁，恐高了以后把双眼蒙着，再把头趴在膝盖上面，那个情景现在我还记得。

整个一片看看应该还不错，他这个小绿蚕没有打，剪枝到明年采摘之后再剪，采完之后再剪。

当时我们接到这个培训任务以后，我们也是很明确的，怎么样培养出一批乡村的骨干，这个是我们的最高目标，我们在后面的整个工作中，我们也都有体会，最难改变的还是人的观念，这个是最大的问题。

In 2018, we came to the village from Tongren City which took us more than four hours. The roads were narrow and were all adjacent to cliffs. Being afraid of heights, we blindfolded ourselves and bowed our heads on our knees. My memory of that trip is still fresh.

The area as a whole looks pretty good. Green silkworms haven't been treated in this tea garden. Pruning can be done after next year's harvest.

When assigned with these training tasks, it was very clear that developing a group of skilled farmers would be our top priority. Throughout the whole process we realized later that the hardest thing to change is people's mindset which can be the biggest obstacle.

【字幕】焦志伟 茶农

Jiao Zhiwei, Tea Grower

【同期】我们祖祖辈辈都是种粮食、种庄稼，一开始说要种白茶，我们心里还有点怀疑，这个究竟能不能成功。

For generations, we've been growing food crops, When we were first told to grow white tea, we were a bit skeptical about whether it would work or not.

【同期】给他讲的时候他听了都懂，但是他后来不按照自己这个老的办法去做，他总归感觉心里面好像没有谱。我们的方法也搞一小点，进行试验一下，一年两年他做过之后，后来胆子大了，他也都会改过来。

When we explained it to him, he understood quite well. However, if he didn't follow his old way of farming, he would later doubt the results. He applied our methods in a small piece of land for pilot testing. After a year or two of experiments, he became more confident, and applied our methods to all his farmland.

【字幕】杨胜强 中寨镇志强村养殖大户

Yang Shengqiang, Farmer, Zhiqiang village of Zhongzhai Town, Guizhou

【同期】他虽然残疾人，但是他能成为首富，我们讲不管他戏称也好不是戏称也好，至少他在自身困难的情况下，他能够这么快的有这个收益，跟他观念的转变确实是不一样的。

Although he's a man with disabilities, he has become the richest man in the village. Jokingly or not, at least, faced with difficulties in life he was able to make a profit so quickly which is a result of his change of mindset.

【同期】从前家中生活条件贫穷，住的是砖瓦房，连家电也没有，自从有了政府帮扶，创办了茶园，帮助我做成之前想做而做不到的事，家庭收入越来越好，也住了小楼房。

同时，也带动大家共同增收致富，把日子越过越好。

I used to live in poverty. My house was tile-roofed. I didn't have any electric appliances. With the government's help, I built my tea plantation. They helped me fulfill my dream which I'd thought was impossible. My family's income is increasing and we now live in a single house. At the same time, the other villagers are motivated to share in the prosperity and enjoy a better life.

【同期】他把手机放给我们看，哪一块茶园随着几月几号修剪的，现在长成什么样子了，他这个手机里面记录全部有。他在学习的时候，

- 193 -

中国式现代化发展之路

应该说是最认真的。

He showed us on his cell phone records of the dates of pruning for each section of the tea plantation, and their current conditions. He keeps all the records in his cell phone. When he was learning, he was very serious and dedicated.

【同期】通过白茶落户过后,这历时三到四年我们已经种了一万零八百亩,这是产业的发展。

Since establishing the white tea plantation, some 10,800 mu of white tea has been planted over three to four years. This is the development of the industry.

【字幕】周应学 中寨镇镇长

Zhou Yingxue, Mayor of Zhongzhai Town

【同期】第二方面就是我们基础设施得到了改善,现在群众的思想转变得到了提升,整体上茶叶种植过后,我们最大的问题就是怎么来管理茶,怎么把茶园、茶苗让它长得好,还有这些病虫害怎么防治。

Second, the local infrastructure has been improved, and the people's mindset has changed. Generally speaking, after the tea is planted the biggest problem is how to manage the tea-planting. How can we make the tea leaves grow well? How can we prevent and control pests and disease?

【同期】现在你们到户以后,把茶叶地里面搞得太干净了。这个茶树你施再多的肥料,它都长不起来。今天主要培训的内容,实际上就是,现在夏季怎么样把这个秋梢长好,包括我们雨水比较多,水土保持的问题,再包括是病虫防治的关键时期,也包括是施肥的关键时期,所以,像这些技术措施怎么样综合进行使用。

我们茶叶做好了,你包括房地产市场、教育市场,很多市场他都能带动,而且他通过积累资金以后,像其他的产业,他都可以做出来,所以你把一个产业做出来以后，实际上是资本的积累、人才的积累。还有这个观念的转变，它这个是一步一步影响整个社会的过程。

When you step into the fields, you'll find that the soil is too clean. No matter how much more fertilizer you add to the tea plants, they won't grow any more. The main topic of today's training is primarily how to prepare the tea plants well for autumn. This includes soil and water conservation during the rainy season, the critical period for pest and disease control and fertilizer application, and how can we combine these technical measures and apply them.

When the tea industry is well established, the markets for real estate, education, and others will all be stimulated. With accumulated capital, other industries may also thrive. When you build up an industry, it helps to accumulate capital and human resources, and it will change people's mindset step by step. It's a process that affects the whole society.

【解说】联合国秘书长古特雷斯曾评价说：中国的精准扶贫是世界扶贫和实现 2030 年可持续发展目标议程的必由之路。政府初始援助是必要的，但中国更强调自力更生。从单纯的"输血"，发展到"输血"与"造血"并重，更是为了避免援助可能造成的依赖性和"精神贫困"。这让我想起道家的一句至理名言："授人以鱼，不如授人以渔"。

Mr. Guterres, the United Nations Secretary-General has said that China's precision poverty alleviation is the only way for the world to help the poor and realize the 2030 Agenda for Sustainable Development Goals. While government assistance is necessary at first, China places greater emphasis on creating self-sufficiency, evolving from mere "blood transfusion" to both "blood transfusion" and "blood creation". This is to avoid the dependency and "spiritual poverty" that direct aids tend to create. This reminds me of a wise Taoist saying which goes "Just giving a man a fish is not as good as teaching him to fish".

【同期】其实我一直想把这个方法推出去，弄完了，写一篇文章，去年入选了十大科技小院的标准模板。

In fact, I've always been thinking of promoting this method. I wrote an article about it. Last year, the idea was among the top ten models for the Science and Technology Backyard (STB) Program.

【字幕】左元梅 中国农业大学资源与环境学院教授 广西隆安火龙果科技小院首席专家

Zuo Yuanmei, Professor, School of Resource and Environment, China Agricultural University, Chief Expert of Science and Technology Backyard Program in Long'an

【同期】我们的这个研究成果到底能给中国的农业解决什么问题，我们更想去验证，我们也发自内心真正地想去帮助农民去解决问题。我们的学科的带头人就是张福锁院士，还有我们李晓林老师，他们当时就是想的就是什么方式把这些创新的技术理论应用到农业生产当中来。就把我们在实验室研究的这些成果，真正地运用到中国的农业生产当中，这就是成立科技小院的一个初衷。

To what extent can our research findings truly solve problems for China's agricultural industry. We are eager to verify the findings and, frankly speaking, we very much want to help farmers to solve problems. The academic leaders of our program are Academician Zhang Fusuo and Mr. Li Xiaolin. What they were considering at that time were the ways to apply innovative technologies and theories to agricultural production and apply the results of our laboratory research to China's agricultural production. This is why we set up the STB.

【解说】左元梅，中国农业大学教授。她所说提到的科技小院，就是由中国农业大学于2009年成立的科技小院项目，一个建立在农业生产一线的科技服务平台。

Zuo Yuanmei is a professor from China Agricultural University. What she is referring to is the Science and Technology Backyard program established by the China Agricultural University in 2009, which is a science and technology service platform established on the front line of agricultural production in China.

【字幕】钟金杏 中国农业大学2021级硕士 广西隆安火龙果科技小院研究员

Zhong Jinxing, Master, China Agricultural University, Researcher of Science and Technology Backyard Program in Long'an

【同期】我是2021级的硕士研究生，在学校学习半年课程之后，在2022年的年初就来到了小院。

I entered the master's degree program in 2021. After half a year's study in the university, I came to the STB at the beginning of 2022.

【字幕】李宝深 中国农业大学资广西隆安火龙果科技小院校外辅导老师 广西农科院科技成果转化专员

Li Baoshen

External Tutor of Science and Technology Backyard Program in Long'an

Scientific and Technological Achievements Transformation Specialist

Guangxi Academy of Agricultural Sciences

【同期】我是当时第一批进驻农业种植企业的研究生，那时候唯一的想法就是，尽快解决香蕉的裂果问题。现在后思极恐，如果2012年的时候裂果问题得不到解决，估计广西的香蕉的品牌可能就砸了。人们当时对肥料简直是一无所知，就只知道肥料是氮、磷、钾，但是对像什么钙、镁、硫、硼、锰，对这些东西几乎是没概念的。

2012年当时刚来的时候，除了解决香蕉的养分管理的问题，还有一个很大的一个隐患，就是香蕉的枯萎病。它其实相当于是香蕉的一个世界级难题，然后我那时候就有一个梦想，希望这个有朝一日，能在我们这一代人里面得到解决，但实际上，十几年过去了，居然我们亲自把它解决了。

2012年的时候香蕉的一个迷茫，到2014年的辉煌，再从2014年到2019年的一个由盛转衰，到2019年以后我们把黄叶病攻克以后，实现一个产业的凤凰涅槃，所以整个过程像过山车一样。

I was one of the first postgraduate students to enter a farming company. At that time, my only wish was to solve the problem of dehiscent fruit in bananas. Looking back, I'm still terrified that if the problem of dehiscent fruit was not solved in 2012, Guangxi's banana brand would have been ruined. People knew nothing about fertilizer except for nitrogen, phosphorus and potassium. They had no ideas about calcium, magnesium, sulfur, boron and manganese. They never considered them.

When I first came here in 2012, apart from nutrient management for bananas, another unforeseen danger was Panama disease, which is actually a worldwide issue. At that time, I had a dream that one day within my generation, the problem can be solved. In fact, after more than a decade we solved the problem ourselves.

In 2012, banana production faced difficulties. In 2014, it prospered greatly. In the following 5 years, it went from a boom to a bust. After 2019, we conquered the Panama disease and the banana industry was reborn. It experienced ups and downs like a roller coaster.

【同期】一开始师兄会带着我到香蕉地里，观察整个香蕉生长过程及操作。在这个过程中，我也学习了解了香蕉的生长规律，那么现在我已经可以自己去采样，回到实验室检测等过程，去检测其中的微生物情况。

百香果它在高温条件下，它很难受花、结果，所以我们通过安装温湿度计进行测温，监测它实时的温度，如果达到了35度以上的高温，我们会进行人工喷淋，进行干预、降温，帮助它在一个合适的环境下开花结果，实现硕果累累的场面。

我想将来能够回到我的家乡，将我在科技小院所学到的技术，进行推广，让我家乡的生活水平变得更加美好。

At first, my senior classmate would take me to the banana field to observe the banana growing process and relevant operations. During the process, I learned to understand the growth pattern of bananas. Now I'm able to take samples by myself and test them in the lab to check for microbial conditions. In high temperatures passion fruit can hardly bloom and bear fruits.

Therefore, we install thermo-hygrometers to measure the temperature and monitor it in real-time. If it gets above 35 degrees, we'll spray water manually to cool it down to ensure the plants bloom and bear fruits in the right conditions. Then, we'll have a good harvest.

I want to go back to my hometown in the future bringing with me the skills I've learned at STB and promote their applications. That will improve the living standard in my hometown.

【同期】这么多年来，我们培养了有20多个科技小院的研究生，我们看到了我们的学生很受社会欢迎。现在我们知道的都已经成为企业重要的技术骨干力量，方方面面发展得很好。他们走向工作岗位以后，他也是心中想着怎么服务三农，真正为农民去解决一些问题。

Over the years, we've trained more than 20 postgraduate students in STB. They are very popular in society. Now some of them have even been serving as the technical backbones of major enterprises. They're doing well in all aspects. When they start to work, they still think about how to serve the farmers, agriculture and rural areas and practically solve problems.

【解说】就这样，在中国各地人们持续为科学技术的进步创造良性的繁育土壤，形成全方位覆盖的发展生态。而有一项科技，它仿佛无形地存在于人们美好生活的每一个角落，极富象征意义，又极具现实价值。

天气逐渐转凉，并将继续过渡到寒冬。曾经，牧民们白天追着羊群跑，晚上还得跑到羊圈中关注产羔母羊的状况，不顾那刺骨寒风。而今天，这里生活已经变得分外惬意。

In this way, all over China, people continue to create a "breeding ground" and all-encompassing development ecology for the progress of science and technology. And there is a technology, which seems to exist invisibly in every corner of people's good life, extremely symbolic, while also of great practical value.

The weather is turning cooler and it will continue to transition into harsh winter. At one time, shepherds ran after their flocks during the day, and at night they had to go to the sheepfolds to pay attention to the condition of the lambing ewes in the biting cold wind. While today, life here has become very cozy.

【字幕】吐尔森·马尔哈旦 村民

Tursun Malahat, Villager

【同期】以前就是找牛的时间，就是十几天、一个星期。现在装了（北斗）以后，不耽误时间，剩下的时间我们自己干活挣钱，好方便了。

In the past, the time it took to find cows was one week or a dozen days. Since we installed (the Beidou navigation system), we don't bother to find the cows. Instead, we can utilize our spare time to make more money. It's very convenient.

【解说】这一切，有赖于依托北斗科技的草原智能监控系统，每一只羊都有定位项圈。北斗系统，通过无线网络把位置传到中继基站，然后送到信息中心，再转送到牧民手持的北斗定位导航和通信终端上。近年来，中国北斗卫星覆盖范围迅速扩大。

2018年底，实现覆盖"一带一路"共建国家。2020年，成功完成了全球组网，实现了全球定位和导航服务。"世界的北斗"已成为现实。

All this depends on the grassland intelligent monitoring system of Beidou Technology. Each sheep has a GPS collar and the Beidou system transmits its position to the relay base station through the wireless network, then to the information center, and finally to the terminal in the shepherd's hand. In recent years, China's Beidou satellite coverage has expanded rapidly.

And by the end of 2018, it had already covered the countries along the Belt and Road, and in 2020, it successfully completed the global networking, making possible global positioning and navigation services.

【字幕】吐尔森·马尔哈旦 村民

Tursun Malahat, Villager

【同期】新时代我们变化就是越来越大，一个手机里面办好多事。这就是我们国家的力量，这就是我们的幸福生活。

Great changes are taking place in the new era. You can do a lot of work using a cell phone. This can be attributed to the power of our country which brings us a happy life.

【解说】今后，它还将继续推动技术创新和合作，推进共同富裕的愿景，为中国乃至全球带来更多的机遇。于是，在今天的中国，我们看到羊群在草原欢快奔跑，又拥有明确的方向。看农民开设网店，销售民族特产。看着养蜂人、遗传学家、医生、庄稼人和清洁工人，都共同踏上了这个国家繁荣昌盛的征程。

当今世界，腐败、战争，不平等的经济和贸易体系依然存在，饥饿依然存在。建立在数百年不公正、不平衡贸易基础上的"输赢"财富观不仅没有解决问题，反而制造了更多的问题，而中国的"共同富裕"理想，为我们这个越来越"小"的星球的现代化，提供了一个可持续的选择。

In the future, it will continue to promote technological innovation and cooperation, advance the vision of common prosperity, and bring more opportunities to both China and the world. In today's China, we see sheep galloping happily in the grassland. And farmers have opened online stores to sell ethnic specialty products. Beekeepers, geneticists, doctors, crop farmers and cleaners all share the same journey into this country's prosperity.

Today in a world still plagued by corruption wars, unequal economic and trade systems and where hunger still exists, the win-lose concept of wealth based on centuries of unjust and imbalanced trade does not solve problems, but rather creates more problems. But the Chinese ideal of Common Prosperity offers a sustainable alternative for modernizing our increasingly small planet.

难以置信的变化：一个美国人眼中的中国式现代化

新华社大型纪录片《难以置信的变化：一个美国人眼中的中国式现代化》之《第三集 上下而求索》

· 中国式现代化发展之路 ·

第三集
上下而求索

【字幕】潘维廉 厦门大学管理学院美籍教授

William N. Brown, Professor, School of Management, Xiamen University (United States)

【解说】北京的胡同带着古老的呼吸,而不远处,就是摩天大楼和繁忙的街道,这是一个融合了古老与现代的城市,很好地体现了中国文化精神所映照出的多样性。当然不仅仅是在这里,在中国的各个角落,协调发展的理念正在深入人心。中国的发展是一个关于平衡的故事,一个关于物质和精神文明共同进步,并相互促进的故事。

Here in Beijing Hutong, alleys exude an aura of antiquity, even though they are surrounded by skyscrapers and bustling streets. It's a blend of the ancient and the modern, a vivid symbol of the diversity reflected in the spirit of Chinese culture. And of course it's not just here, but in all corners of China, that the idea of coordinated development is emerging. It is a story of balance, of material and spiritual resonance and their mutual promotion.

【字幕】难以置信的变化——一个美国人眼中的中国式现代化

Incredible Transformation—Chinese Modernization through the Eyes of an American

第三集　上下而求索

Far, Far was the journey

【解说】2008年，中国人口最多的省份之一四川，发生了特大地震。15年过去了，这里的人们还好吗？

In 2008, Sichuan, one of China's most populous provinces, was hit by a catastrophic earthquake. Fifteen years later, how are the people here?

【字幕】杨华珍　国家级"羌绣"传承人

Yang Huazhen, National-Level Inheritor of Qiang Embroidery

【同期】2008年"5·12"大地震的时候，好多的志愿者送物资，还有解放军送药进去，全国人都在过来捐款捐物。我怎么来帮我家乡呢？我就想到了，我有手艺，我的针线活不错。我就想，我们走出大山，去寻找手艺，凭手艺挣回来的钱来建设我们的家园。

After the earthquake on May 12, 2008, many volunteers donated supplies to my hometown alongside the People's Liberation Army which transported medicines. People from all over the country donated money and materials. What can I do for my hometown? Then I thought of my craftsman skills. I'm good at embroidery. So I thought that we could leave the mountains and earn money with craftsmanship. With the money we earned, we could rebuild our homes.

【解说】杨华珍出生于四川省的一个藏族村寨。她从小就帮着妈妈做针线活，到十六的时候，已经凭着自己的刺绣手艺，在家乡小有名气。杨华珍虽然一直把刺绣作为自己的爱好，却没想过，要靠此做一番事业。

Yang Huazhen was born in a Tibetan village in Sichuan Province. She has been helping her mother with needlework since she was a child. By the time she was sixteen, she was already well known in her hometown for her embroidery skills. Yang has always regarded embroidery as her hobby. However, she has never thought of making a career out of it.

【同期】我就自发地,组织了十八个老姐姐,一半有藏族,一半是羌族。我们就组织起来,走出大山,我们说去闯荡江湖。

So I invited 18 women to set up a work team. Half of them are Tibetans and the others are Qiang people. We decided to head out of the mountains. We started a journey to run our business.

【解说】从一个摄影师,到一个创业团队的领队人。她意识到创业没有她当初想的那么简单。

From a photo journalist to the leader of a start-up business, she realized that being an entrepreneur is not as easy as she first thought.

【同期】我当时工资一个月有三千多,靠我的工资买菜买米,我怕那些姐姐饿肚子,还有她们的安全。我就压力有点大,我就后悔了,后悔了,晚上我就哭了,结果闯荡江湖不简单,混不下去了。

有一天接到一个电话,一个老总,他说我有一个宾馆,你帮我宾馆里面,你说怎么装饰软装就怎么装饰,我就开始设计。法国的一家宾馆,就看到绣品跟宾馆结合,软装是很好,实用性强,一下提升了宾馆(的装饰艺术),广告就打出去了。一次订单、二次订单……一桶金、二桶金……我们就起来了,我们就发财了。

At that time, my salary was over 3,000 yuan a month. I bought food for the team with my salary. I was concerned about their food supply and their safety. I was under a lot of pressure. I regretted deeply. I cried at night. It turned out that running a business was not easy. We couldn't make it.

One day I got a call from a businessman. He told me that he had a hotel that he wanted me to decorate, saying I may design the interior as I wish. So I started designing. It's a hotel in France, I thought that embroidery may fit the hotel well. Embroidery is good for interior decorating. It's very practical and the hotel interior has been greatly improved. Our brand soon grew. We received many orders in a row, and gradually made money, Our business was a success which brought us good wealth.

【解说】成功不是偶然，靠的还是真本事。

Success is not a coincidence. It's based on real skill.

【同期】前几天香港赛马，出了一匹黑马，是冠军。他们说可不可以，在手表里面表现，我说我争取，我来试试。原来我才知道，真的是民族的才是世界的，还有传统的才是时尚的。

我现在专门会去拜访山上的老艺人，去挖掘几百年、上千年一代一代传承下来的东西，是好东西，我相信这一点。坚持就是胜利，文化就是自信。

A few days ago in a horse race in Hong Kong, a dark horse became the winner. I was asked whether the result could be presented on a watch dial. "Let's try it," I said. "I'll do my best."

Then I realized that what's folk is also global, and that the traditional can be fashionable.

Now I pay special visits to old craftsmen in the mountains to discover hundreds and even thousands of years old craftsmanship that has been passed down from generation to generation. It's valuable. I believe in it. Perseverance leads to victory. Culture gives us confidence.

【解说】今天，在中国各地，璀璨的艺术文化遗产，正以这种样的方式承载着中华民族的智慧和创造力，铸就丰盛的物质文明。

·中国式现代化发展之路·

In China today, people are carrying the wisdom and creativity of the Chinese nation rooted in rich cultural legacies to create astounding wealth for the country.

【字幕】潘维廉 厦门大学管理学院美籍教授

William N. Brown, Professor, School of Management, Xiamen University (United States)

【解说】现代中国的奇妙魅力在于,在每个人的日常生活细节中,古代与现代是如此自然和谐地共存。它能在灾难之后给人们带来希望,并将现代体育与古老民间风俗融合,发展出惊人的中国式创新。

The charm of modern China is that the ancient and the modern coexist so naturally and harmoniously in the details of everyone's daily life. This can give people hope after a disaster or help them blend modern sports with ancient folk customs to evolve cutting-edge Chinese innovations.

【字幕】贵州省 黔东南州 榕江县

Rongjiang County, Qiandongnan Prefecture, Guizhou Province

【解说】在中国的贵州省——榕江县,每周六晚上都会举行一场不同村寨之间的足球比赛。它被称为"村超",是诙谐效仿国际足球联赛而命名,"村超"由当地村民创建,参与者主要是村民。

现年49岁的杨亚江,是当地一所小学的校长。他既是比赛发起人之一,又是场上队长,还是赛事的协调员。

A soccer game among different villages in Rongjiang county, west China's Guizhou Province is held on every Saturday evening. The Village Super League, "Cun Chao", humorously named after those international soccer league tournaments was created by local villagers, and the participants are mainly villagers.

Yang Yajiang a 49-year-old principal at a local elementary school, was one of the game's initiators and field captain, and on-site coordinator as well.

【字幕】杨亚江 贵州省榕江县足协副主席 车民小学校长

Yang Yajiang, Vice Chairman of Rongjiang County Football Association, Guizhou, Principal of Che Min Primary School

【同期】29号那天我负责，我们千人唱侗族大歌的节目的组织，特别是各村各寨的演员一些联络。

On the 29th I organized a performance of 1,000 people singing songs of the Dong ethnic group, especially the contact with each village and their actors.

【同期】好的，观众朋友们。贵州榕江村超比赛的最终决赛，现在开始了。

Dear friends, the final of the Village Super League of Rongjiang, Guizhou now begins.

【解说】这场比赛很接地气，迅速火爆社交网络，甚至吸引了足球巨星迈克尔·欧文的关注，他还录制了一段视频以示支持。

The match is so down-to-earth that it became an instant hit on social media. It has attracted the attention of football legend Michael Owen who recorded a video to show his support.

【解说】现场解说杨兵，成为社交网络的名人。其实，他的日常身份是当地一家银行的行长。

Yang Bing, the match commentator, went viral on social media. Actually he is a director of a local bank.

【字幕】杨兵 "村超" 解说员 中国建设银行天柱支行行长

Yang Bing, Match Commentator of the "Village Super League", Director, Tianzhu Branch, China Construction Bank

- 209 -

·中国式现代化发展之路·

【同期】我们村超当时也没有现场解说，老百姓来球场看球了，气氛不是那么好。老百姓只是看，想着能不能解说，调动下气氛。就这样很意外地就走到了解说席，就拿着话筒开始讲。老百姓发自内心的全面参与，38万多人，老百姓对村超带来的那种精神愉悦，就可以体现在他们的脸上，更多能体现着我们的民族的一个自信，我们文化的一个自信。

We didn't have any live commentary at that time. The people came to watch the game but they were not excited. They were just watching. I wondered if live commentary might warm up the atmosphere. So I went to the commentator's booth, picked up the microphone and started commentating. The locals participated enthusiastically, representing a total population of over 380,000 in the county. That kind of spiritual pleasure gained from the Village Super League is reflected on people's happy faces. It also reflects people's confidence in our nation and our culture.

【同期】我们最大的目标就是，通过举办乡村足球赛，能够让整个黔东南的，整个贵州省的，甚至全世界的爱好足球的朋友到榕江来，更能够有效地去交流足球，把各自的一些民族文化，拿到榕江来更好的一些展示，让全世界的朋友就像石榴籽那样紧紧地拥抱在一起。

Our ultimate goal is that by organizing village football matches football fans across southeastern Guizhou, across the province and even across the whole world, will come to Rongjiang, to share their passion for football. Meanwhile, they may bring their own cultures to Rongjiang to demonstrate. Let friends all over the world hug each other, as tightly as pomegranate seeds.

【解说】激烈的比赛和有趣的民族风俗表演，让"村超"成为贵州一个独特的文化符号。还带动了以体育为核心的文旅经济发展，以体育为核心的文旅经济发展。

The exciting games and ethnic art performances have made the Village Super League a unique cultural symbol of Guizhou. It has also led to the development of a sports-centered cultural and tourism economy.

【同期】我们这里他不光男孩喜欢足球，女孩也特别的喜欢足球，包括我们各村各寨都会有女足。现在我们各个学校，都开展女足的训练和教育。踢球更多的就是给我们带来快乐和幸福。

Not only boys love football here. Girls love it too. We have women's football teams in every village. Today, all our schools provide training for female football players. Football brings us joy and happiness.

【同期】因为我们口寨村进了八强，所以昨天 7 月 30 日，我们村的村民，自发的，杀牛、杀猪，来给球队庆功，真的很感谢。我们口寨队得到村民的支持是我们最大的动力。

Because our Kouzhai Village team entered the quarterfinals yesterday, on July 30, people in our village spontaneously butchered cattle and prepared nice food to celebrate the team's success. We're really grateful because our Kouzhai Village team gained the most strength from the support of our villages.

【解说】是体育运动的魅力，还是古老文明的凝聚力，使"村超"大获成功，我们不必刻意区分。内心的丰盈，已经成为人们应对复杂多变生活的立足点。

这个国家的人民，正在努力将传统智慧与现代进步相结合。他们以更大的自信心和主动性，激发古老文明的活力，开创更加生机勃勃的未来。

Whether it is the appeal of sports or the cohesion of an ancient culture that makes the difference, there's no need for us to make a distinction. Inner abundance has become the anchor point for coping with the complexities and changes of our life today.

The people of this country are working to combine the wisdom of tradition with the advances of modernity. And with greater self-confidence and initiative, they are applying the vitality of their ancient civilization to forge an even more vibrant future.

【解说】上个世纪，由于种种原因，许多中华文明遗存流落海外。如今，一些中国学者正试图重新找回失落的中华文明瑰宝。

Over the past century, for various reasons, many relics of Chinese civilization were transferred overseas. Today, some Chinese scholars are trying to bring these lost treasures home to China.

【字幕】王小松 浙江大学艺术与考古学院副院长

Wang Xiaosong, Vice Dean, School of Art and Archaeology, Zhejiang University

【同期】民国初年，五老图及部分题跋被分割转售，流落到海外。"中国历代绘画大系"工程的规划与实施，为了追寻散外在（海外的）名迹，提供了重要的机遇。

In the early days of the Republic of China, the painting Five Elders and some of the inscriptions were divided and transferred overseas. The Chinese Paintings through the Ages project offers a great opportunity to track the paintings scattered overseas.

【解说】2005年，中国国家级重大文化工程，中国历代绘画大系工程正式启动，意在为中国古代画作建立精准的数字化档案。

In 2005, a major national cultural project called the Chinese Paintings through the Ages project was launched, with the intention of bringing together ancient Chinese paintings to create an accurate digital archive

【同期】这些名画时间很久远，很多细节已经难以看清，但通过我们数字化放大，以及用高清的扫描，所以完全可以满足非常苛刻的研究条件，大概能够放大300倍，就能看到非常的清晰，就能从中能感觉到古人那种独具匠心的画家卓越的这种功力。

Those paintings are very old and many of their details are hard to identify. But we used digital enlargement techniques and high-definition scanning to meet such demanding needs of research. With about 300 times of enlargement, details of the paintings can be much more easily seen. Thereby, we can appreciate the ingenuity of esteemed artists from ancient times.

【解说】然而，许多物品很难收集，它们不仅数量有限，而且散落在世界各地。

However, many items are difficult to collect. They are not only limited in number but also scattered all over the world.

【字幕】金晓明 浙江大学中国古代书画研究中心副主任

Jin Xiaoming, Deputy Director of the Research Center of Ancient Chinese Calligraphy and Painting, Zhejiang University

【同期】有些收藏单位，一件作品的拍摄，可能要持续好多年的讨论、申请，甚至是反复去。比如说黑川古文化研究所的《寒林重汀图》，我们去了四次才拍完。

In some cases, photographing a single work may require years of negotiations and applications and even multiple visits. For example, the painting Wintry Groves and Layered Banks collected by the Kurokawa Institute of Ancient Cultures in Japan took us four trips to photograph.

【解说】为了让这些文物"回家"，学者们把眼光放眼全球，开展了3次全球图像搜集，走遍全球260海外文博馆，历经成千上万次的通讯联络和寻访行程。

To help these cultural relics return home, scholars have shared their vision globally. Three global image collections have traveled the world to over 260 overseas museums with tens of thousands of communications and hundreds of thousands of trips.

· 中国式现代化发展之路 ·

【同期】它（"大系"）对于中国传统文化，走向世界，让世界的相关的艺术史界、学术界，以及世界的一些喜欢中国文化和艺术的百姓，来认识中国文化，是有借鉴意义的。

最近两年我们做了一些普及性的，巡回展览工作，那么多的不一定是喜欢画画，不一定是学画画的人，就是普通的百姓，蜂拥而至，都要来看这个东西。

The Chinese Paintings through the Ages project is important as it presents traditional Chinese culture to the world. It provides an opportunity for people in the art and academia, and people around the world who like Chinese culture and art to learn more about Chinese culture through these masterpieces.

In the past two years, we organized traveling exhibitions to promote these works of art. So many people, not necessarily those who like to paint or learn to paint, but just ordinary people came in large numbers to see the paintings.

【解说】这些努力不仅仅为古老绘画带来新生，更激发了人们在文化领域的创造性变革。在开放包容，为世界提供了一个古老文明与现代创新共生共荣的典范。今天，中国人的自信心和成就感与日俱增。

Such an effort not only brings new life to ancient arts but also inspires creative change and innovative development, and provides the world with a model of co-prosperity between ancient culture and modern innovation. Today, the Chinese people's self-confidence and sense of achievement is growing.

【字幕】潘维廉 厦门大学管理学院美籍教授

William N. Brown, Professor, School of Management, Xiamen University (United States)

【解说】而实际上，这也是对中国古代思想家朴素愿景的追溯，"仓廪实而知礼节，衣食足而知荣辱。"300年前，一位英国政治家尤斯塔斯巴杰尔写道：中国最伟大的成就，不是四大发明，而是"精确治理的艺术"。这种精准治理方式,从中国古代的愿景和价值观中演变而来,今天仍然是中国现代化行稳致远的关键。

Yet in reality, this is simply a restoration of ancient Chinese thinkers' simple vision of "being well provided for in the granary knowing the proprieties and etiquette, being well clothed and well fed and knowing honor and disgrace."

300 years ago, an English politician Eustace Budgell wrote that China's greatest achievement was not its four great inventions, but its "art of government". This precision way of government evolved from ancient China's vision and values and today is still the key to the stability of Chinese modernization.

· 中国式现代化发展之路 ·

新华社大型纪录片《难以置信的变化——一个美国人眼中的中国式现代化》之

《第四集 天地我同根》

难以置信的变化
——一个美国人眼中的中国式现代化
Incredible Transformation--
Chinese Modernization through the Eyes of an American

第四集 天地我同根
All Things With Me

第四集

天地我同根

【字幕】潘维廉 厦门大学管理学院美籍教授

William N. Brown, Professor, School of Management, Xiamen University (United States)

【解说】孔庙坐落于北京城市中心地带，是为纪念中国古代伟大思想家孔子而建。孔子以及众多中国古代哲学家都强调顺应自然，比如道家的创始人老子就说过"道法自然"。在中国，我最喜欢的古代生态案例是有着 2200 年历史的都江堰水利工程，它在不限制河流自然流量的情况下，使四川成为中国西部的粮仓。在环境问题上，尽管过去几十年中国走过弯路，但它保护环境的决心坚定不移。

This Confucius Temple in the heart of Beijing was built in honor of Confucius, the great thinker of ancient China. And Confucius and other ancient Chinese philosophers emphasis working with nature. For example, Laozi, father of Taoism, said "Man follows nature". My favorite example is the 2,200-year-old Dujiangyan irrigation which to this day makes Sichuan West China's breadbasket, without restricting the river's natural flow. To this day, China's emphasis on protecting the life-giving earth is unwavering despite some detours over recent decades.

【字幕】难以置信的变化——一个美国人眼中的中国式现代化

Incredible Transformation—Chinese Modernization through the Eyes of an American

第四集　天地我同根

All things with me

【字幕】1994 年 嘉峪关，2019 年 嘉峪关

1994 Jiayu Pass, the Great Wall, 2019 Jiayu Pass, the Great Wall

【解说】这两张照片我拍摄于同一个地方，位于中国西部戈壁沙漠边缘的嘉峪关市。1994 年的嘉峪关遍地黄沙，而 2019 年的这张照片上，这里已经是满眼绿色。近年来，中国不断加强全方位的生物多样性保护体系建设，设立了 23 万平方公里国家公园。位于中国西部四川境内高山峻岭之间的大熊猫国家公园就是其中之一。

I took these two photos over 20 years apart in the same place in Jiayuguan, a city on the edge of West China's Desert. This area was all sand in 1994, but in 2019 it was green, and even had a lush forest nearby. In recent years, to strengthen its holistic biodiversity protection system, China has established 230,000 square kilometers of national parks, including the Giant Panda National Park, in the mountains of West China's Sichuan Province.

【字幕】四川 雅安 宝兴县

Baoying County, Ya'an, Sichuan

【同期】工作内容第一个就是护林防火，野生动物保护，还有（监督）非林开垦，乱采林地。比方说乱采、乱挖这些，现在，正当在搞这个职业、搞绿化，里面要栽树子，最困难就是出去了之后下大暴雨这些，你上山这些也比较困难。比方说你要去看野生动物有没有问题，有些地方过都过不去。

My job involves forest protection, fire prevention, wildlife protection, and the monitoring of reclamation activities such as the indiscriminate exploitation of forest land. For example, people may conduct quarrying and digging. Now in the protected areas reforestation is carried out, and trees are planted. The hardest part is getting caught in a rainstorm when working outside. Then it can be difficult to climb the mountains. When I need to check whether there're problems with the wildlife, I cannot even enter some areas.

【解说】从未离开过这片大山，59岁的护林员但召辉。这里是宝兴县，地处中国西部四川盆地西部边缘，紧邻青藏高原。

7月进入汛期后，这里发生多处泥石流，阻断了但召辉日常的巡山工作。这几天，情况好转，他准备再次进山巡护。

Dan Zhaohui, a 59-year-old ranger, has never left these mountains. This is Baoxing County, located on the western edge of the Sichuan Basin, in western China close to the Qinghai-Xizang Plateau.

In July when the flood season began, mudslides interrupted Dan's daily patrols. Over the past few days, the situation has improved and he is preparing to venture back into the mountains for his patrol duties.

【字幕】但召辉 四川省宝兴县林业局管护员

Dan Zhaohui, Conservator of Baoxing County Forestry Bureau, Sichuan

【同期】自从退耕还林以后，我们这里的宝兴县生态还是很好的。以前比如说是荒坡，现在栽起竹子了，很好的。保护野生动植物，老百姓的思想觉悟是很高的，我们搞保护这些野生动物，保护这些树木并不是说我们愿意把它保护起来，而是我们把它保护好了为子孙后代。

Since the return of farmland to forest, we've been enjoying a good ecological environment in Baoxing. In the past, some slopes were barren, but now bamboo is planted there. It's very good. People are well aware of protecting wildlife. We protect the wildlife and the trees not simply for their own sake but also for future generations.

【解说】说到野生动物，这里跟其他地方相比非常特别，因为这里是中国特有的珍稀动物大熊猫的家乡。1869年法国传教士阿尔芒·戴维，在这里第一次见到大熊猫。他的发现在西方世界引起轰动，大熊猫，黑白相间的皮毛非常独特，它不仅是充满魅力的形象标识，更是中国秘境里多样的生态网络的象征。由于建立了大熊猫保护基地，像但召辉这样的昔日伐木工人，已成为如今的国家公园生命守护者。

When it comes to wildlife, these mountains are very special compared to others because it is the home of China's unique and treasured animal the giant panda. It was here that French missionary Pierre Armand David first saw a giant panda in 1869 and his discovery caused a sensation in the Western world. The giant panda with its distinctive black and white coat is not just a charismatic icon, but a symbol of the intricate web of life that thrives in China's remote regions.

Thanks to the Panda Protection Base, former lumberjacks like Dan have become guardians of life in this national park.

【同期】身体不舒服、不健康，那么就它的粪便是稀的，相当稀。熊猫很健康的话，那个结结是一坨坨的，它屙出来是整的。如果说是拉稀，你就要看，这个熊猫就走不远，就在这一块儿活动。

If a panda falls ill, its feces are thinner. If it is healthy, the feces are more solid and come out complete. If the feces are thin, you'll find that the panda cannot walk far away and is still nearby.

【解说】今天，护林员已经采用了先进的红外照相机，来获取大熊猫的远程无线传输影像数据。

Today, rangers have adopted advanced infrared cameras to obtain remote wireless transmission of giant pandas' image data.

【同期】它这个就是一个兽道，这个兽道比较陡，它从下面上来的话才能把它看清楚。如果说安高了的话，就看不清楚。这个天线就是把拍到的东西发射过去，那边的基站直接传送到电脑里头，电脑里头就显示出来了。

This is an animal path which is quite steep. The monitor can capture clear images of the animal coming up. If the monitor is installed too high, it cannot capture clear images. This antenna will transmit what the monitor captures. Then the base station will transmit data directly to the computers, which display the images.

【同期】这是一头成年的黑熊（黑熊猫），气力是相当大。这儿全部都给它掏空了。如果说你发现它了，你要去接近它，你慢慢去，你不要跑过去，它以为你要去打它，它就要跑。

This is an adult black panda which is very powerful, and hollowed out the tree trunk here. If you see the panda and want to approach it, you should do it slowly rather than run at it or it may think that you're trying to attack it, and then it will run away.

【解说】对待野生大熊猫，要以保护野生动物的野性，不破坏自然发展规律为原则。但遇到特殊情况，还是要有必要的救助。

The protection of wild pandas should be based on the principle of maintaining the wild nature of wild animals and not destroying the laws of natural development. However, there are still special circumstances that call for necessary assistance.

·中国式现代化发展之路·

【同期】大熊猫在鱼通沟救了一个。他们早上是9点就给我说，我上去就把它找到了。

We once rescued a panda in Yutonggou valley. They messaged me at 9 o'clock in the morning. I reached the area and found the panda.

【字幕】运送被救助大熊猫去治疗

Transporting rescued pandas for treatment.

【同期】请了10个人，才把这个熊猫装在笼子里面。这个熊猫得了白内障。它最后拉在碧峰峡去治疗，最后说还是健康的。比方说野生动物也多，森林保护好了，为子孙后代留一个，现在要求的是金山银山，绿水青山。

Ten people worked together to put the panda in a cage. The panda had cataracts. It was later taken to Bifengxia Panda Base for treatment. Finally, it recovered. With diverse wildlife and well-protected forests, we may present future generations with invaluable assets of lucid waters and lush mountains.

【解说】大熊猫的生存故事显示，今天在我们的星球上，人与自然的脆弱关系已经恶化到了严重的地步，也同时显示，困境又是如何在中国得以持续修复。现代社会的发展令人与自然的微妙关系变得愈发紧张。我们对能源的依赖，再加上对环境造成的改变，导致了意想不到的后果。气候变化提醒我们，维护我们与地球的关系，需要尊重和有效管理。

我们再不能想当然认为自然给予我们的赐福能够永远存在。对于这一点，中国人再一次提出了有效的解决方案。

The story of the panda's survival shows that our small planet's fragile relationship between humans and nature has deteriorated to a serious point and also how China is methodically addressing this problem step by step. Our modern pursuits have strained humanity's delicate relationship with nature.

Our reliance on energy coupled with the alteration of our environment has led to unintended consequences. Climate change serves as a reminder that our connection with the Earth demands respect and stewardship.

We can no longer take for granted that nature's blessings will last forever. Here too the Chinese have come up with an effective solution.

【字幕】山西 天镇旭升光伏电站

Shanxi, Tianzhen Xusheng Photovoltaic Power Station

【解说】光伏，是如今最普遍的绿色能源之一。当前，中国拥有世界上最大的光伏发电规模。这样的变化，在山西这个中国重要的煤炭出产省份，尤其令人印象深刻。在山西天镇，以光伏产业为中心，一幅美丽的生态图景正在成型。

Solar power is one of the most prevalent green energy sources today and China currently possesses the world's largest scale of solar power generation. Such changes are particularly impressive in Shanxi, an important coal-producing province in China. Here in Tianzhen, Shanxi, a beautiful ecological scene centered on the solar energy industry has taken shape.

【字幕】刘怀亮 晋能清洁能源光伏发电有限责任公司总工程师

Liu Huailiang, Chief Engineer, Jinneng Clean Energy Solar Power Generation Co., LTD

【同期】这个光伏电站选址，它一般都是选在这个荒地和盐碱地这个未利用地的上面。咱们做了一个光伏电站以后，组件对这个地表面做了一个遮挡，遮挡以后下雨以后，蒸发量小了，它保湿情况比较好，反而是对绿色植被啊草呀，生长环境比较有利。

Solar power stations are usually built on barren land, or saline land, which have not been utilized. After the solar power station is built, the modules shade the surface of the land. When it rains, the evaporation rate is smaller and the land retains moisture better. Green vegetation such as grass will enjoy a more favorable environment.

【同期】而且就是说这个野生动物也比较多了，这可能是形成了一个小的这个小的一个生物链群体了。

The number of wildlife is also increasing and it may have developed into a small ecosystem.

【字幕】天镇村民

Tianzhen Villager

【同期】自从这个光伏电站建设以来，对我们村里面，挺好的。生活水平都提高了。

Since the construction of the solar power station, our village has benefited a lot. Our living standards were improved.

【字幕】王蛟龙 天镇旭升光伏电站站长

Wang Jiaolong, Director, Tianzhen Xusheng Solar Power Station

【同期】这个项目为其他地区提供了一个可行的模式，激励更多地方投资绿色能源，并倡导可持续的生活方式。电站不仅仅是一个能源项目，更是一项对环保意识的教育，为未来的可持续发展奠定了坚实的基础。

This project has provided a viable model for other areas, inspiring more places to invest in green energy and promote sustainable lifestyles. The power plant is not only an energy project, but it also helps to raise environmental awareness which lays a solid foundation for sustainable development in the future.

【解说】天镇旭升光伏电站，总装机规模245兆瓦，占地面积约4.5平方公里，相当于560个标准英式足球场。如何保障光伏持续稳定发电量，成为这里的科技工作者必须面对的问题。

Tianzhen Xusheng solar power station, with a total installed capacity of 245 megawatts, covers an area of about 4.5 square kilometers, equivalent to 560 standard soccer fields. How to guarantee the continuous and stable power generation of solar power has become a difficult problem that the scientists and technicians here must face.

【字幕】王蛟龙 天镇旭升光伏电站站长

Wang Jiaolong, Director, Tianzhen Xusheng Solar Power Station

【同期】旭升光伏电站占地是6,775亩，它的光伏组件就有905,595块。如果说是光靠人工去把这些工作全部排查一遍的话，那可能半年才能下来。

Xusheng Solar Power Station covers an area of 6,775 mu and consists of 905,595 photovoltaic modules. If manual labor is used to check all the modules, it would take half a year.

【同期】我们配的这个人少，主要是我们采用了一些比较先进的一些技术手段，那实际上让我们采取这个机器人巡检。

Our team is quite small and we complete our work mainly using advanced technologies. Robots are used for inspecting the modules.

【同期】用于发现光伏组件热斑情况，去发现这个潜在的一些隐患。

It helps us to detect hot spots on the modules and other potential hazards.

【解说】现在，这一片深蓝色的太阳能电池板，已成为当地的独特风景，是这片荒山荒坡上的生态经济希望。

Today, this patch of dark blue solar panels has become a unique local landscape. They have become the ecological and economic hope on this once barren slope.

【同期】它能足够保证咱天镇县，所有的社会居民、工业一年都有电量。我们这个天镇旭升光伏电站总装机是24.5万千瓦，它全年的发电

· 中国式现代化发展之路 ·

量是 3.8 亿度。对于光伏和火电来对比，全年可节约标煤是 11.45 万吨。可以减少 31.5 万吨二氧化碳的排放。

The power from the station is sufficient for our county's residential and industrial use every year. The solar power station has an installed capacity of 245,000 kW, which generates 380 million kWh of electricity per year. Compared with thermal power stations, the solar power station saves 114,500 tons of standard coal each year and reduces 315,000 tons of carbon dioxide emissions.

【解说】在广阔的宇宙中，我们与太阳的关系，引发了我们对于自身在宇宙中位置的思考。古代文明曾奉太阳为神明，但今天，我们对太阳本质的理解已经发生了变化，揭示着太阳与人类之间深刻的相互联系。在中国的所见提醒我，当我们站在责任的十字路口上时，我们应记住，我们与太阳的关系不仅仅是物理上的互动，更在深刻提醒着我们去认识自身在生命体系之中的意义，呼唤我们拥抱生态智慧，分担责任，维护我们脆弱的小星球的微妙平衡。

In the expanse of the universe, our relationship with the sun invites contemplation of our place in the cosmos. Ancient civilizations once worshipped the sun as a deity, but today our understanding of the sun's nature has evolved, revealing a profound interconnectedness. What I've seen in China reminds me that we stand at the crossroads of responsibility. Our connection to the sun is more than a physical interaction. It is a profound reminder of our place in the intricate web of life, calling us to embrace ecological wisdom and to share responsibility for maintaining the delicate balance of our fragile little planet.

【字幕】三峡集团福建海上风电场 全球首台 16 兆瓦海上风电机组

Three Gorges Group Fujian Offshore Wind Farm, The world's first 16 MW offshore wind turbine

【解说】今天，中国坚定走自己的方向，大力推进绿色、低碳发展，为绿色发展提供清洁、可持续的能源解决方案。自古以来，中国人就将人与自然视为一个整体，人类的幸福与自然息息相关。在今天的中国，保护环境已经从一种古老的智慧演变成一种文化，一种坚定不移的潮流。我想，中国近年来在生态保护方面取得的巨大成功也表明，环境不只是政治问题，同时也是生命意义本身。这恰恰是中国式现代化中人与自然和谐相处的理念核心。

Today, China is firmly heading in its own direction promoting green and low-carbon development and providing clean, and sustainable energy solutions for green development. Since ancient times, Chinese have viewed human and nature as a holistic entity and human happiness is closely related to nature. In today's China, protecting the environment has evolved from an ancient wisdom to a culture and an unwavering trend. I think China's great success in ecological protection in recent years also shows that the environmental issue is not just political, but also life itself. And this is precisely the core of the concept of harmony between humans and nature adopted by the Chinese path to modernization.

·中国式现代化发展之路·

新华社大型纪录片《难以置信的变化：一个美国人眼中的中国式现代化》之
《第五集 相知无远近》

第五集

相知无远近

【字幕】潘维廉 厦门大学管理学院美籍教授
Professor, School of Management, Xiamen University (United States)

【解说】我爱这片海,不仅因为它的蔚蓝和宁静,也不仅因为海岸线上多姿多彩的风景,还因为它的辽阔和永不停息的潮汐,提醒着我为什么来到这里,以及我走过了多远的路。在遥远的古代,太平洋的波涛中出现了一条隐秘的丝绸之路。中国古代海上丝绸之路,从这里,它承载着来自东方的宝藏和智慧,连接着不同文明的心灵。各国的商人和航海家,成为和平的使者,他们共同分享财富,更重要的是他们把理解和信任编织成和平的织锦。

I love this sea, not only for its azure color and peacefulness or the colorful landscapes along the coastline, but also for its vastness and the endless tides that remind me of why I am here and how far I have traveled. In distant ancient times, a hidden silk road emerged amidst the waves of the Pacific Sea—the ancient maritime Silk Road of China. From here, it carried treasures and wisdom from the East connecting hearts of different civilizations. Traders and navigators from many nations became messengers of peace. Side by side they shared wealth and more importantly wove threads of understanding and trust into the tapestry of peace.

【字幕】难以置信的变化——一个美国人眼中的中国式现代化

Incredible Transformation—Chinese Modernization through the Eyes of an American

第五集　相知无远近

All for one, one for all

【解说】苏勇来自老挝，他曾经是北京林业大学留学生，专业是森林遗传与林木育种。

Phangthavong Souksamone is from Laos and was an international student at Beijing Forestry University specializing in forest genetics and tree breeding.

【字幕】苏勇　教师　老挝籍

Phangthavong Souksamone, Teacher (Laos)

【同期】我是2013年到中国，汉语水平考试，考过了我就第二年才可以上专业课。到2017年，毕业以后我就回家，回家在老挝找工作，在农业的大学（一个农业大学）当老师。

I came to China in 2013. I needed to pass the Chinese Proficiency Test before I could take specialized courses the following year. In 2017, I went back to Laos after graduation and looked for a job there. Then I became a teacher at an agricultural university.

【解说】而他持续关注着中国的发展，希望继续把中国的技术带回老挝。2023年，机会来了，他参加了中国商务部主办的技术培训班，重返中国。

And he continued to follow China's development hoping to continue to bring Chinese technology back to Laos. In 2023, the opportunity came. He attended a technical training course organized by the Chinese Ministry of Commerce and returned to China.

【字幕】广东 正旭现代农业孵化园

Zhengxu Modern Agriculture Incubation Park, Guangdong

【同期】今天我也学了剪枝，学了荔枝相关知识，感觉非常好。我们来参观培育，四个国家一起来的，老挝、越南、泰国和尼泊尔。在这里我们有十几个人，我们有不同的想法，可以互相分享交流。

Today I learned how to trim branches and learned a lot regarding lychees. I feel great. We came to observe the lychee cultivation process. The members of our group are from four different countries, Laos, Vietnam, Thailand and Nepal. There are more than ten of us visiting the farm. We each have different ideas and we can share our ideas with each other.

【字幕】苏勇 教师 老挝籍

Phangthavong Souksamone, Teacher (Laos)

【同期】那个照片很有用的，是因为，我们回去的时候也可以把这个照片用在幻灯片，或者讲给我们国家人看一下，在中国的荔枝园是这样的，很有用的。平时荔枝的种子挺大的，但是他们可以做那个简单的基因，不让荔枝的种子大，让荔枝的种子小。这样的，非常好的。

Photos are particularly useful. You see when we go back, we can display the photos in slide shows or show them to our fellow people, showing them how the lychee gardens in China look. It's very useful. Usually the lychee seeds are very big, but they can apply a simple genetic modification to limit the size of the lychee seeds and make them smaller. That's what they do. It's a very good idea.

中国式现代化发展之路

【同期】最甜的（品种）是桂味

The sweetest variety of lychee is Guiwei.

【同期】中国和老挝荔枝方面可以交流，是因为我们那里品种很少，没有中国的丰富，而且中国的品种也很好的。我们可以拿中国的荔枝品种去老挝种一下，有可能效果也很好。我打算是带这里的经验回去老挝那里，分享这个经验给我们的学生，我们的农村人那里，怎么种荔枝，怎么管理荔枝，将来我也打算，再回来北京继续读博士。

China and Laos can exchange lychee cultivation techniques. We have fewer lychee varieties in Laos. China's lychee varieties are also really good. We may take some of China's lychee varieties and plant them in Laos. The result might turn out very good. I intend to take China's experience back to Laos, share it with our students and rural people and show them how to grow lychees and care for them. I plan to come back to Beijing for my PhD.

【解说】600年前，中国明朝著名航海家郑和七下西洋，他的行程远至非洲海岸。他史诗般的航旅故事激发了辛巴达故事的灵感，也促进了中非之间的友谊与合作。今天，这样历史遗产正焕发出新的活力。一位雄心勃勃的企业家，千里迢迢来到中国，探索这个充满活力和创新的国家。在这里，摩天大楼拔地而起，技术与商业相互交织，创造出一个吸引世界目光和想象力的现代奇迹。

600 years ago, Admiral Zheng He, the renowned Ming Dynasty Chinese mariner whose seven epic voyages inspired the tales of Sinbad, sailed as far as the shores of Africa. Zheng He fostered a spirit of friendship and cooperation between the two realms. Today, this historical heritage is sending out new shoots. An ambitious entrepreneur took thousands of miles to China to explore this dynamic and innovative country. Here, skyscrapers rise and technology and commerce intertwine to create a modern marvel that has captured the world's attention and imagination.

【字幕】广东 塔米姆家中

Ahmed Tamim's Home in Guangzhou

【解说】坦桑尼亚商人塔米姆，已经在广州打拼了13年。

Tamim is a Tanzanian businessman who has been working in Guangzhou city for 13 years.

【同期】我的第一个生意是冰激凌生意。

My first business is the ice cream business.

【字幕】艾哈迈德·塔米姆 坦桑尼亚籍商人

Ahmed Tamim, Tanzanian Businessman (Tanzania)

【同期】因为我那时是无名小卒，没有钱，当时的生意只够糊口，没有再多了，但也养活了我们，我、我妈妈和我身边的其他人。后来我换了行业开始卖二手手机，这是我在坦桑尼亚的最后一个生意。后来我一个兄弟或者说我老板，他叫我来中国。你知道2010年时，没有多少人了解中国，尤其是在非洲国家，没有多少人了解中国。

Back then I was nobody with no money. The money I earned was enough just for food and nothing more. But me, my mom and people around me made a living out of it. I changed my business to sell second-hand mobile. This is my last business in Tanzania. Then my brother or my boss called me to come to China. You know back in 2010 not many people knew China, especially in African countries, not many people knew about China.

【解说】2006年，中非贸易额首次超过500亿美元。与此同时许多中非货运公司成立，天生有商业头脑的塔米姆，不会放过这个机遇。2010年，他来到了广州。

In 2006, China-Africa trade exceeded $50 billion for the first time. At the same time many China-Africa freight companies were established. Tamim who

中国式现代化发展之路

was born with a business mind would not let go of this opportunity and in 2010 he arrived in Guangzhou.

【同期】我刚来西轮海运公司的时候,我是一个打包工,普通工人。我操作这样的机器,在中国两三年以后,我看到了许多的机会。

When I started in Silent Ocean, I was a normal compressing worker. I operated this machine. After two years or three years in China, I've seen many opportunities.

【同期】这是什么?短裤。这些短裤可以踢足球时穿。一些非洲人会当做内裤

What's this? Short pants. You can wear these for football. Some African people use them as underwear.

【同期】关于中国我什么都想知道。

I want to know everything about China.

【字幕】艾哈迈德·塔米姆 坦桑尼亚籍商人

Ahmed Tamim, Tanzanian Businessman (Tanzania)

【同期】我将了解如何在中国做生意。在当时,许多非洲人会想来中国太难了。怎么找到一个工厂?怎么下订单?如何在中国做生意?非常难。所以我会花时间,去试着连接起中国和坦桑尼亚,中国和非洲的关系,一起做生意。

I wanted to do business in China. Back then, many African people thought it was very difficult to come to China. How to find a factory? How to make order? How to do business in China? It is very difficult. So I will use my time to try to connect between China and Tanzania, China and Africa to make business together.

【同期】有时我会邀请一些中国朋友来看看我的文化,比如要是有

非洲人的聚会就邀请来，就邀请他们来看看我的文化，品尝我们的饮食等等，我们将彼此文化交融。

Sometimes I invite some Chinese friends to see my culture, like invite them to an African party, see my culture, taste our food. We mix our culture.

【解说】如今，凭借诚信和勤奋，塔米姆已成为广州坦桑尼亚商会的主席。诚信、勤劳、利他，也是中国现代化发展中与全世界的朋友交往的准则，这种双赢的现代化方式，强调的不是一方的快速获利，而是所有参与者的长期获利，和平是唯一可持续的道路，中国已将这一理念，进一步转化为非凡的科学愿景。

Today, thanks to integrity and hard work, Tamim is the chairman of the Tanzanian Chamber of Commerce in Guangzhou. Integrity, hard work and altruism are also the guidelines for China's modernization and development interactions with friends all over the world. This win-win modernization approach emphasizes not fast profits for one party, but long-term profits for all participants. Peace is the only sustainable path. China has further translated this vision into a marvelous scientific vision.

【同期】记者 5 号从中国天眼 FAST 运行和发展中心获悉

According to China's FAST Operation and Development Center.

【字幕】贵州 平塘县 克度镇航龙文化园

Hanglong Cultural Park, Kedu Town, Pingtang County, Guizhou Province

【同期】中国天眼 FAST，2021 年将迎来它面向全球科学界开放第一年。4 月 1 号开始，接收来自全球科学家的天文观测申请，预计分配百分之十的观测时间给国外科学家。

The year 2021 will mark the start of its opening to the global scientific community. On April 1st, it will begin accepting observation applications worldwide. 10% of the total observation time is expected to be allocated to international scientists.

【解说】FAST是中国自行研制的，世界上最大的单口径射电望远镜，与美国的"凤凰"计划相比，它将类太阳恒星的考察目标至少扩大了5倍。

China's FAST is the world's largest single-aperture radio telescope. Compared with the United States' "Phoenix" program, it will expand the targets of sun-like star inspections by at least five-fold.

【字幕】姜鹏 "中国天眼"总工程师

Jiang Peng, Chief Engineer, FAST Program

【同期】FAST发现脉冲星数量，应该是同一时期国际上，所有其他望远镜发现脉冲星总数的三倍以上，所以从这个来讲，也是充分证明它在的灵敏度方面领先能力。

The pulsars detected by FAST in the same given period worldwide is more than three times the total of pulsars detected by all other telescopes. In this sense, it's fully evident that FAST is an advanced leading player in observation sensitivity.

【解说】FAST从建设之初，就制定了逐步向世界开放的原则。随着国际合作的开展，迄今为止它已经发现了800多颗新的脉冲星，探测到宇宙中最强的爆发信号，快速射电暴，实现超长基线干涉测量。首次在射电波段观测到黑洞"脉搏"。如今，它的加速运行已经开始，这将为全人类的全面发展，提供源源不断的动力。

FAST已成为一件非凡的巨型科技艺术品，透过历史的尘埃，凝望星空深处，致力于为人类共同的未来，带来无限的探索和思考。

From the very beginning of its construction, FAST has emphasized a gradual opening-up to the world. As international cooperation has developed, FAST has discovered over 800 new pulsars, detected the strongest outburst signals in the universe—fast radio bursts, and realized the ultra-long baseline interferometry. And for the first time, it observed the "pulse" of a black hole in the radio waveband. Today, it has begun accelerated operation which will provide a constant impetus for the comprehensive development of all humanity.

FAST has become an extraordinary giant technological work of art, gazing into the depths of the stars through the dust of history, dedicated to bringing infinite exploration and contemplation to the common future of mankind.

如今，已有14个国家的27份国际项目，获得批准并启动科学观测。这也彰显出，中国对全球科学发展的责任与担当和坚持和平发展的意愿，而中国式现代化所憧憬的未来，就是要打破对外扩张掠夺的现代化老路，顺应人类发展进步的时代潮流。

Today, 27 international projects from 14 countries have been approved. This demonstrates China's commitment to its global scientific responsibilities and serves as a testament to China's peaceful intentions. The future envisioned by Chinese modernization is to break the old path of modernization of foreign expansion and plundering and to conform to the epochal trend of human progress.

中国"一带一路"倡议提出十年来，取得卓越成就。

In the 10 years since China's Belt and Road Initiative was put forward, remarkable achievements have been made.

【字幕】中老铁路

China-Laos Railway

【解说】在中国的帮助下，老挝人民的铁路梦成为现实。

With China's help, the Laotian people's dream of railroads has become a reality.

【字幕】柬埔寨金港高速公路

·中国式现代化发展之路·

Phnom Penh-Sihanoukville Expressway, Cambodia

【解说】柬埔寨进入"高速公路时代"。

Cambodia has entered the "highway era".

【字幕】马尔代夫跨海大桥

China-Maldives Friendship Bridge, Maldives

【解说】马尔代夫有了跨海大桥。

The Maldives has a cross-sea bridge.

【字幕】吉利汽车白俄罗斯本地化生产

Localized Production of Geely Cars in Belarus

【解说】白俄罗斯有了自己的轿车制造业。

Belarus has its own car manufacturing industry.

【字幕】非洲亚吉铁路

Addis Ababa–Djibouti Railway

【解说】非洲有了电气化铁路和轻轨。

And there are electrified railroads and light railways in Africa.

【解说】展望未来，中国将进一步加强同世界各国的共赢合作。为世界和平与发展作出更大贡献。

Looking to the future, China will further strengthen win-win cooperation with other countries around the world and make a greater contribution to world peace and development.

【字幕】潘维廉 厦门大学管理学院美籍教授

William N. Brown, Professor, School of Management, Xiamen University (United States)

【解说】这片海见证了世界的变迁，也常常给我以启迪。一望无际的潮水，古老的庙宇，繁华的城市，无不散发着诱人的光芒。这是一个不仅与世界分享古老智慧的国家，也是一个愿意与世界携手共创真挚友谊与和平未来的国家。

This sea has witnessed the changes of the world and often inspires me. The endless tides, the ancient temples, the bustling cities all exude an inviting light. This is a country that not only shares its ancient wisdom with the world, but is also willing to work with the world for a future of heartfelt friendship and peace.

纪录片组成员

钱　彤、崔　峰、傅　琰、肖思思、马逸群

邓驰旻、刘　阳、汤　阳、王　科、熊　琦

薛　晨、胡玥聪、刘音苑、付　敏